East of the Atlantic West of the Congo

ART FROM EQUATORIAL AFRICA

THE
DWIGHT AND
BLOSSOM STRONG
COLLECTION

Leon Siroto

Kathleen Berrin, Editor

THE FINE ARTS MUSEUMS OF SAN FRANCISCO
Distributed by THE UNIVERSITY OF WASHINGTON PRESS

This catalogue has been published in conjunction with the exhibition *East of the Atlantic, West of the Congo: Art from Equatorial Africa from The Dwight and Blossom Strong Collection.*

The Fine Arts Museums of San Francisco
M. H. de Young Memorial Museum
15 July–26 November 1995

Published with the assistance of The Andrew W. Mellon Foundation Endowment for Publications.
Copyright 1995 The Fine Arts Museums of San Francisco

Distributed by the University of Washington Press, P.O. Box 50096, Seattle, WA 98145.

Library of Congress Cataloging-in-Publication Data

Siroto, Leon
    East of the Atlantic, West of the Congo : art from Equatorial Africa from the
Dwight and Blossom Strong Collection / Leon Siroto; Kathleen Berrin, editor.
        p.   cm.
    Exhibition catalog.
    Includes bibliographical references.
    ISBN 0-88401-080-5
    1. Decorative arts, Black—Africa, French-speaking Equatorial—Exhibitions. 2. Strong, Dwight—
Art collections—Exhibitions. 3. Strong, Blossom— Art collections—Exhibitions. 4. Decorative arts—
Private collections—United States—Exhibitions. I. Berrin, Kathleen. II. Fine Arts Museum of San
Francisco. III. Title.
NK1087.3.S57   1995
730'.09672'07479461—dc20   95-12537
                                                            CIP

Front cover
FACE MASK (detail), cat. no. 16

Title page
TOBACCO PIPE (detail), cat. no. 48

Printed and bound in Hong Kong.

CONTENTS

PREFACE

ithin the span of just two decades Dwight and Blossom Strong have created a focused and distinctive collection of the arts of Western Equatorial Africa. The collection is not a comprehensive view of all the arts of this vast region—for no collection could be, given the tremendous vitality and variability of this little-understood culture area. Nor does the collection focus on "classics" in Gabonese art, although the classics are certainly present. Many of the objects in the Strong Collection are intriguing precisely because they are not the well-known object types that collectors find appealing. This is one of the characteristics that make this collection a source of surprise and fascination.

The Strong Collection reminds us that African art cannot be approached simplistically, nor with the view that the arts can be precisely understood or easily categorized. Problems in the scholarship of the arts of Western Equatorial Africa have been and continue to be especially acute, owing to the absence of solid field studies over time. The lack of dependable historic and cultural information about the peoples of Western Equatorial Africa has made it difficult to understand their amazingly varied art traditions, especially those of the peoples of central Gabon, about whom so little has been written. It is hoped that this publication will articulate some of the difficulties of the past and perhaps even stimulate new directions in scholarship.

Because projects such as this are always a collaborative effort, we wish to thank many. Dwight and Blossom Strong deserve special thanks for their generosity, kindness, enthusiasm, and willingness to share their collection. Leon Siroto, a noted specialist in the ethnology and art of Western Equatorial Africa, has not only provided the majority of insightful remarks that appear here but also knows the objects extremely well, having served as long-time advisor to the Strongs in the formation of their collection. Alisa LaGamma, a scholar in the arts of the Punu who currently holds the Jane and Morgan Whitney Fellowship at The Metropolitan Museum of Art in New York, has been a valued advisor. The appearance of the publication owes much to the following individuals: Kaz Tsuruta, a talented and painstaking photographer, is responsible for the many striking images; Desne Border was a meticulous copy editor; and Robin Weiss gave the book its notable design. The work was published with the assistance of The Andrew W. Mellon Foundation Endowment for Publications.

On The Fine Arts Museums staff, Ann Karlstrom, Director of Publications and Graphic Design, and Karen Kevorkian, Editor, have been indispensable in the planning and production of this publication. Ellen C. Hvatum Werner, Assistant Curator to the Department of Africa, Oceania, and the Americas, has provided considerable support for curatorial aspects of the project. Eileen Petersen, Executive Secretary, worked tirelessly to prepare the manuscript. We wish to thank the many other dedicated members of our museum staff who have combined their special talents, expertise, and skills to realize this catalogue and exhibition.

HARRY S. PARKER III
Director of Museums

KATHLEEN BERRIN
Curator, Africa, Oceania, and the Americas

Collectors' Acknowledgments

Many people have had a part in forming our collection and the events leading to its exhibition. Two who must be specially thanked are Director Harry Parker and Curator Kathleen Berrin. Under their leadership, the staff of The Fine Arts Museums of San Francisco has mounted the exhibition and formed the catalogue in a way to make us proud. Two other people have had a special part in forming the collection: Dr. Leon Siroto and Mr. Irwin Hersey. Mainly out of friendship and fellowship, they have helped us to determine what is interesting and pertinent. We are grateful to them for much inspiration and for leading us to many good things in our collection.

DWIGHT AND BLOSSOM STRONG

REFLECTIONS ON THE SCULPTURE OF A REGION

THE DWIGHT AND BLOSSOM STRONG COLLECTION

Leon Siroto

Not long after Dwight Strong began to collect African traditional art in the late 1970s, he became aware that his relatively late start would limit him to acquisitions that were modest in regard to fame and fortune. He therefore deemed it prudent to collect in order to tell rather than to show—to use his collection to make points that went beyond the expectations and reservations of the art-collecting milieu.

This led to a plan to bring together images from just one part of sub-Saharan Africa; at the outset he considered the nation of Gabon only. Learning that I was an anthropologist with a special interest in the ethnology and art of Gabon, Strong invited me to take part in the building of a collection that would contribute to a greater understanding of that nation's art in relation to its own background and, incidentally, to its interpretation from the Western cultural perspective.

I had one initial reservation: because so much of the art and culture history in question went beyond the borders of Gabon, it would be advisable to extend our frame to take in Western Equatorial Africa. The art and the culture history of the region involve the peoples of at least five nations: Cameroun, Gabon, Equatorial Guinea, the People's Republic of the Congo, and the Central African Republic. My fieldwork among the Kwele[1] of both the People's Republic of the Congo and Gabon made this regional perspective the only reasonable one.

THE LAND AND ITS PEOPLES IN THE 1800S

The wide extent and special features of this region make difficult the use of a more succinct term than Western Equatorial Africa. On the map it descends from about 5° north latitude to 5° south latitude and goes across from about 5° to 17° east longitude. Its natural boundaries are the Atlantic Ocean, the Wuri and Sanaga Rivers, the Middle Congo River, and the Kouilou

River (not the Kwilu of southwestern Zaire and adjacent Angola). Most of the region inland rises above sea level; its lower parts occur along the coast and larger rivers. Many of the rivers do not allow ascent by vessels, and thus important trade to the coast has been limited. Rain forest prevails over the north, while a mixture of savanna and woodland characterizes the south and parts of the east.

Aside from some Eastern Nigritic enclaves (Ngbaka- and Banda-related groups) in the north and east, Bantu speakers have accounted for the village population of all the region.[2] They often lived in symbiosis with bands of spear- or net-hunting pygmies. Village societies depended on shifting cultivation of the staple crops, which allowed them to migrate through and occupy the forest.

Reports by European travelers of the last century find corroboration in ethnographic data and African oral tradition gleaned in this century. These early statements acquaint us with the region's turbulent history through the latter part of the eighteenth century and most of the nineteenth century. This period saw great, albeit gradual, movements of Bantu speakers in a prevailing north-to-south direction, which soon became especially significant as they turned westward toward the coast.

The reasons for this massive shift were varied; they included internal population growth and the awareness of wonderful foreign wares arriving at the coast. Other Bantu speakers had already settled on the Atlantic Coast and in the relatively open country below the northern forest well before these upheavals. This is evident in the intense interaction between the Portuguese navigators and missionaries and the Kongo-speaking kingdoms to the immediate south of the region, during the sixteenth and seventeenth centuries.

Over those centuries the coastal trade determined much of the history of the region. European traders exchanged such highly desirable items as brass, copper, iron tools, cloth, beads, and buttons against the ivory, plant products, and slaves coming to the coastal peoples from the interior. In turn, the inland peoples received their payment in European goods from their coastal partners. The rarity of this merchandise gave it great value in the traditional bride-wealth systems.

The commercial activity of groups, both settled and newly arrived on the coast, expressed itself in a cult that carried competition to the supernatural level, offering fortune to those who followed rites that included the use of family relics and guardian statues. These observances seem to have begun on the coast, in the days before more powerful families assumed control of trade through systems of centralized, ascribed leadership. The cult, in its broad sense, probably followed the trade network eastward, from the Ngumba through the Beti and some Fang, and from the eastern Kele speakers (Ngom and Shekiani) through other Fang and the Kwele, undergoing reinterpretation as it diffused.

Change of this sort was important to the regional development of traditional religions that used art. Yet, such change worked against preserving the details of that development for Western scholars, who would now wish to understand the relationships between lending-and-borrowing societies in this connection. Research along these lines comes up against a lack of information on the forms and styles of religious imagery in use among the peoples whom the later migrants encountered as they progressed southward.

The little information at hand—mainly from Du Chaillu[3]—suggests that

38 STANDING FEMALE
FIGURE
An undetermined people (Punu,
Mbama, Nzebi, Tsaangi or Kunyi);
southwestern People's Republic of
the Congo; 20th century
Wood, pigment, fiber, and resin
21 x 7¼ in. (53.5 x 18.5 cm)

In the southwestern People's
Republic of the Congo a number
of unrelated groups follow, at least
partly, Shira-Punu style. The head
of this figure shows that affinity, but
the angularity of its body and limbs
might undercut that correspondence.
Further departure from Shira-Punu
style, or that of the Kongo-speaking
peoples who have strongly influenced
the Shira-Punu, is evident in the lid-
like section apparently sewn into the
front of the torso, the cord covered
with resinous substance. This concept recalls the reliquary figures of
the Mbete speakers; some of these
groups are geographically close to
those who follow Shira-Punu mask
style in the southwestern People's
Republic of the Congo. ("Mbama" is
not to be confused with "Mbamba"—
each is a distinct group name.)

the western Kele speakers supplanted by the Fang and Kwele had more tech-
nically advanced cultures than those of their successors. We learn that the
pattern of their culture agreed substantially with that of peoples studied
carefully during this century, but only rarely have examples of their art
come to us clearly identified.

Dedicated hunters and traders, the western Kele speakers inhabited much
of the region in small, widely dispersed units, often in enclaves within the
nominal territories of societies more given to cultivation. They may have
enjoyed some importance as a cultural "connective tissue" between those
peoples, transmitting innovations from one to the other. Limited available
information suggests both some attainment in their religious art and some
concern to preserve its secrecy against European inquiry.

This historical lack of witnesses has encouraged the questionable notion
that the traditional arts of peoples who now characterize the region were both
primal and peculiar. This facile assumption has allowed lay participants in
the attributions of this region's art forms to oversimplify discourse on the
ethnic and cultural backgrounds of available images.

A far too clear-cut picture of this region's art history emerges from most
of the specialized publications that the field accepts as authoritative. It often
leads to the fallacy of reading culture and history from art alone, as in the
assumption that a large ethnic group that produced cult statues now realizing
great market value conceived their sculptural style independently of the
influence of smaller neighboring groups, who had observed the same cult
for a longer time. The Strong Collection illustrates numerous reasons to be
wary of accepting specious dogma.

According to the documented history of this region, the peoples involved
in this trade had attained an appreciable level of affluence in the essentials
of life: dependable and abundant staple crops, a usually sufficient supply of
meat in wild game and small livestock, and a store of adequate tools replen-
ished by a mastery of iron smelting and forging. The main commodities they
sought conferred temporal power—guns and brass, the latter important in
marriage payments; supernatural power—the use of metal, beads, and buttons
to adorn guardian statues in order to enlist and enhance their power; and
personal prestige—attained through adornment with valuable and beautiful
materials.

Between 1880 and 1930 colonial occupation and administration put an
end to the indigenous trade networks. National borders divided previously
integral ethnic groups, leading to their increased interaction with unrelated
groups and to subsequent changes in their cultures. Administrative expedi-
ents hastened false assumptions about the primal and cultural relationships
between ethnic groups and their art traditions.

Thus colonial authority and missionary zeal sent into obsolescence most
of the older cults that employed images. Indigenous witch-hunting movements saw to the destruction and abandonment of the old cult accessories.
After a hiatus in the 1920s, master carvers, who had supplied these cults
with masks and statues, discovered a new demand for their skills. French
and Spanish colonial officials and entrepreneurs learned of the prices that
traditional images commanded on the Western art market. Carving for
Europeans provided one of the few enjoyable ways to earn the cash needed
in a vastly changed economy.

The rise in market value attained by traditional art from Western Equatorial Africa began in the 1910s, concomitant with the ascendancy of the paintings of the School of Paris, especially those of its cubist phase. Many styles of the region showed striking relationships (not always coincidental) to the styles of the leading French artists of the period. At first the masks and reliquary guardians proved desirable as a complementary decorative effect in collections and exhibitions of paintings. Not long afterward they gained a cachet of their own.[4]

Through this period, representatives of French art dealers made sweeps, both intensive and extensive, through the region—mainly among the Fang and the so-called Kota peoples. "Intensive," in this respect, denotes an element of great haste. The acquisition of the material seems to have taken place without any recording of its nature and background other than, say, *Idole pahouine, Gabon* (Fang idol, Gabon). The sectors, ethnic groups, villages, and carvers from which these many images came are now lost to us.

WESTERN PERSPECTIVES ON THE ART OF A REGION

Yet the wholesale transportation of images to Europe as merchandise did prove fortunate in rescuing an important corpus from the abandonment that in this region leads quickly to decay. The gain in terms of preservation is, however, somewhat offset by a loss in accessibility. Sold piecemeal, the images have often ended up scattered widely and obscurely through museums and private collections in the West. It seems likely that some aesthetic surprises await us in the occasional bobbing up of a remarkable unknown example at an auction or a gallery, and, just as likely, this kind of epiphany will not include revelation of the circumstantial details available when the object was about to go west.

This lack of evidence has occasioned stratagems for the localization of traditional images after the fact of their precipitous intercontinental transfer. Some scholars have undertaken style monographs using received ideas of culture history applied to a predominantly undocumented corpus of images. The most ambitious and widely accepted of these is a classification of Fang reliquary guardian statuary by Louis Perrois that seeks to connect sculptural form with the aesthetic preferences of ethnic subdivisions.[5]

Perrois's method depends on charting patterns of body proportion across a sampling of statues assigned to the regional groups that make up the Fang entity. This mechanistic approach led to categories demonstrating canons that determined attenuation, squatness, and the intervening gradations of form. Although the discussion included tables of such diagnostic details as coiffure, body adornment, and pose, these features did not significantly enter into the determination of the subgroup styles; this led to instances in which variation in proportion assigned statues in the same style to different categories.

This approach has its shortcomings. The almost total lack of data concerning the precise origin of the statues undercuts any claim to rigor in the procedure. The so-called ethnic subgroups can vary in name and number from one authority to another. No focused study of the subject has shown the extent of their significant differences. They appear to be connected with Fang precolonial history and with some regional identity, but this, especially among the Fang, would not imply any hermetic quality in their cultures.

Among the few authorities qualified to comment on Fang traditional art, the anthropologists James and Renate Fernandez published in 1975 a telling critique of the Perrois thesis,[6] pointing out the complexities of Fang history and social organization that stand in the way of any absolute assignment of an undocumented statue in an unfamiliar style to any particular local group.

Four years later, Alain and Françoise Chaffin published a formal classification of the styles of metal-covered reliquary guardian figures attributed to such Kota speakers as the Ndasa and Wumbu, and such Mbete speakers as the Mbamba and Ndumbo.[7] While their method resembled that of Perrois, they worked more with features than proportions. The simple and flat forms of these images easily fell into homogeneous and elegant groupings, except for some gratuitous compounding according to the convexity or concavity of the faces of figures in essentially the same style. In effect, the study served as the preparation of a corpus for eventual localization. In most cases, the authors chose not to connect distinctive form with any particular ethnic or local group. Data of origin are as deficient for these Kota images as they are for the Fang.

Not surprisingly, soon after the 1972 publication of the Perrois monograph, its findings were widely and unreservedly accepted. It attained international recognition as the definitive guide to Fang sculptural styles, one that could provide short and simple labels to expedite nonspecialist discourse. The vocabulary diffused vertically as well as horizontally, from authors to college instructors to leading ethnologists and art historians.

Into this hasty enlistment in a system of belief can be read a relatively new and specialized discipline's need for a stopgap jargon to account for the significant-seeming differences between objects continually gaining in value and fame. One might have expected this new terminology to have remained tentative until further data and a more humanistic way of looking at form could lead to revision. Circumstance, however, worked to protect the Perrois overview; the Fernandez article was the last detailed challenge to its validity.

The door closed on the subject; the premise became a given; and one of the most remarkable assemblages of traditional African statuary remains firmly divided into self-contradictory and, to some, untenable groupings. This is not to say that a more definitive and valid arrangement may be feasible, but only to suggest that the corpus be unbound to gravitate into natural clusters determined by the features special to artists and schools—even if the data of origin never emerge.

My discussion of this expression of Western engagement with the art history of this region goes beyond the challenge to its soundness. Much of the knowledge about this art comes from sources that cannot be challenged, either because they cannot be found or because they fall outside of the professional field, disclaiming ultimate responsibility for what they publish or otherwise communicate.

The art of this region has not attracted a significant number of serious students in search of disinterested understanding. This lack has allowed the field to develop into an odd mixture of sound scholarship and undemonstrated claims issuing from the shadows of the marketplace. Dealers and art prospectors, whose names often remain unknown, pursue their quest for stock through little-studied ethnic groups. They gather and record names and ask leading questions about religion, working these glancing inquiries into romantic variations on the great themes of popular anthropology. These amateur impressions can find their way into the unwitting texts of museum publications and auction catalogues, where the printed word imbues them with authority. In effect, information—whether valid or misleading—on this region's traditional art seems to be hardening into a code which will not, or cannot, accommodate the reality accessible through overlooked perspectives and premises.

Overlying a thin layer of early Western travelers' observations of African art at its source, there is a comparatively substantial body of received expertise about the object itself, rather than its reflection of ethnic and societal contexts. Belief in this reductive principle flourishes among sellers and buyers of art who assume that continual contact with a foreign and obscure art form will eventually lead to an infallible intuition as to which examples are "right" and which "wrong."

From this vantage point, "right" is a matter of form and finish conforming with those of the earlier examples to come on the market and pass through a sequence of illustrious owners. By this standard an image can be "wrong" simply by its failure to agree with a canon of style established from afar, casually, and in the interest of commerce. Thus a work of unfamiliar style or features may be unlikely to attain the pedigree that familiarity would ensure.

This dogma has its corollaries. An "authentic" mask or statue should show clear signs of "ritual use," implying that its maker worked in profound religious faith and that his clients used his work in religious dances and solemn rites. The element of tradition expected in this evaluation would provide assurance that the object be as old as possible—which, in the absence of historical records or internal evidence, would suggest an analogy to the fame and value of classical antiquities.

My comments in regard to this art-collecting milieu are greatly simplified in order to point out a cultural pattern that tends to limit our knowledge of styles and iconographic types. Many sculpturally and art-historically significant images lose their allure as they run the gauntlet set up by the art market. Failing to move the orthodox, they drift toward the margins of the collecting scene. Arbitrarily named according to the established style they might resemble, acquired as curiosities and conversation pieces until their authenticity is challenged (as it always is), they return to the market in cycles until they drop from sight. Their marginality often results more from obscurity of background than aesthetic shortcoming. Such ambiguity represents a risk to investment and reputation.

Many images in this category—valid-seeming works of some artistic quality or explanatory interest—fall in between the better-represented and more fashionable styles recognized by the market. The Strong Collection's

42 PROBABLY A COLUMN FINIAL

An undetermined people, possibly Ngom or Ngom related; western Gabon; possibly ca. 1900
Wood, pigment, and metal
15¼ x 3½ in. (38.5 x 9 cm)

The Ngom and their Kele-speaking relatives were the most important people living behind the coast of north and central Gabon before the advent of the Fang. As suppliers of forest products to the Myene on the coast they partook of the wealth brought in by European trade. They had a number of sculptural styles, one of which seems to correspond to that of the maskoids on the top of this column. The Ngom maintained fortified men's houses through precolonial times. This object may have been part of a once-higher column erected in the men's house as a rack for hunting implements and ritual paraphernalia. The antennaelike processes rising from the top do not seem sturdy enough to have served any architectural purpose.

importance lies in its core of such free-floating works, rescued from obscurity by recourse to overlooked contextual information and by fortunate insights into formal correspondences.

This range of images should indicate something about the reasoning that consigns indeterminate styles to supposedly determinate ones and conceals simple and foreseeable cultural change behind constructions of romantic fantasy. Facile judgments on the nature of the region's traditional arts derive in part from corresponding cultural patterns in other areas of Western and Central Africa.

Certain givens—supraregional patterns developed distinctively in Western Equatorial Africa—are prime determinants of the cultural systems that use imagery in this region. Their differentiation reflects the historical circumstances of massive migrations inland, generally from the savanna into the forest, and the impact of European contact, notably in trade, along the coast through the nineteenth century.

Leadership

Large centralized systems of ascribed, or hereditary, leadership prevailed in the south, reflecting Kongo and Teke influence, and on the coast, reflecting the great effect of European trade. Elsewhere, political organization was manifest in the leadership of local hereditary chiefs who were often family chiefs as well. Most of the ethnic groups followed a rule of consensus, in which the society's elders had to reach a decision jointly in matters affecting their families. These egalitarian systems were primarily local. They provided a field for interfamily and intervillage competition, which often expressed itself in the use of more or less secular forms of imagery in order to attain societal prestige. Striking effects in the insignia of status and in personal adornment served to reflect prestige and to indicate leadership.

The Men's House

Although it is a cultural feature that appears, in essence, in many societies outside the region, the men's house may have attained its highest development, in terms of decoration, in Western Equatorial Africa. As far as records show, however, exceptional examples were rare. The occurrence of showpieces seems confined to the times of migration and trade, which greatly distinguished the history of the region.

This structure provided a fixed place for the men of a community to come together under shelter to pursue such affairs as discussion of policy, litigation, communal eating, reception of guests, practice of crafts, and performance of ritual. In many societies its building plan did not differ much from that of the dwelling house; in its most contrastive form it resembled an open-sided hangar.

In the northern part of the region—among Yaunde-Fang speakers, Makaa-Njem speakers, and Kele speakers—the men's house sharply defined the space of a minimal lineage group of fathers, their sons, and the families of both, all under the leadership of the eldest or the most competent father.

Villages usually consisted of a number of lineage units marked by the presence of a men's house in the middle of each segment. Through the nineteenth century, these buildings were, in effect, guardhouses charged with defending the village against trespass. Walled mainly by upright logs, rather than plates of bark, their structure and exterior surface were stark and pragmatic. Within, however, a wide range of decorative techniques—often varying by region and ethnic group—contributed to the prestige of its owners.

The main pillars provided a field for sculpture in the round, relief carving, openwork effects, and poly-chromy (cat. no. 43). The posts that held weapons and packets of various kinds shared this sculptural treatment (cat. no. 42). Along the walls ran beds and benches with decorated props or frames of vividly col-ored bark plates. The red, black, and white geometrical patterns showed considerable variety in texture brought out by hollow relief, applied elements, and a sort of cloisonné in which strips of cane separated spaces of contrasting colors.

Very little of this kind of decoration was collected for museums or the art market, nor has the subject received much attention since Tessmann's time.[8] We cannot assume that the practice occurred in every society or even in every lineage within a society. It certainly was part of the concern with prestige, and at its most spectacular it would have reflected the power and wealth of a lineage chief with the many followers needed to realize a great and doubtless renowned house. In 1960–61 the Kwele responded to my ques-tions about differences in the care of their villages and persons, their skill in crafts, and the interpretation of ritual by answering, invariably, "That depends upon the family."

In the mountains of central Gabon, where the Ogowe River has kept northern incursions from com-ing through en masse, the Tsogho and their neighbors enjoyed relatively peaceful circumstances through traditional times in the nineteenth century. There the men's house developed in a different way, but still showed—and perhaps surpassed—the artistic enhancement characteristic of the warring peoples to the north. The families constituting a village pooled their resources and built one large communal cult house to hold the sacred objects used in cele-brating the rites of their cult of family relics.

The great cult house—regarded as a kind of temple by colonial administra-tors—was a large, oblong, partly open-sided building accessible through entrances at its short sides. In front the central pillar and the shorter, flanking ones that supported the eaves were usually carved in one way or another, often with polychromed human figures fashioned in the round (cat. no. 41).

Distinctive among the effects of this cult were stelalike planks (cat. no. 40) that served as the jambs of a frame setting the lateral limits of the sacred space of a provisional altar used in certain rites, such as mourning. A trans-verse panel set toward the tops of the jambs defined the upper limit of the framed space. These elements represented mythological beings in the Tsogho

myth of creation. The elements differed greatly in detail: some figures surmounting the jambs were flat, others three-dimensional. They were usually figurated; polychromed geometric motifs were an invariable feature of their decoration.[9]

Ancestor Spirits

Belief in the existence and power of the spirits of dead relatives is widespread, if not universal, through sub-Saharan Africa. Such belief is expressed in many different ways, among them the cult of ancestors. The term *ancestor* has not been clearly defined in its pragmatic sense by anthropologists or students of religion working in Africa. Western culture perceives ancestors at a considerable remove in time and not likely to affect the lives of their descendants.

In many African views, the cult of ancestors sought to use the power of the recently deceased—especially those who had great power imputed to them when they were alive—to mediate between them and the world of nature spirits. Because this power was believed to be transient, the cult focus would continually turn to the spirits of the next generation of the dead.

Nature Spirits

Complementary to the belief in the spirits of ancestors was an awareness of the natural world as a realm of unseen beings associated with cosmic phenomena, local places, plants, animals, and the fortunes of humankind. Partly by virtue of their precedence in the world, these spirits had greater powers than those of men, either living or deceased. Thus, men sought to enlist their aid as tutelaries by embodying them in images (including masks, often showing animal attributes) and in nonrepresentational symbolic assemblages somewhat analogous to chemical formulas. Cults of the family dead believed that their ancestral spirits could intervene on their behalf with the spirits of the world of nature.[10]

THE RELIQUARY CULT

The peoples long established on the coast gained wealth through a thriving trade with Europeans. They and their partners inland would have attributed their success to the proper traditional magic. Trade magic using family relics was so widespread among the peoples just behind the coast that it may well have originated on the coast. The religious premise focused on the bones of a deceased relative, particularly the skull, as a source of power in the quest for wealth, through both European trade and the indigenous marriage system, the wealth units of which that trade had affected.

The cult of family relics attained its most notable development in this region. Its ritual practices were distinctive, its iconography unique. It is possible that it diffused into the region from Kongo speakers to the south. Its transmission from the coast into the interior was, given its underlying motivation, remarkably rapid, passing from one ethnic group to the next for payment, thus becoming an item of commerce in itself.

Because of its wide range in this region, the system of belief in the supernatural power inherent in relics came to be known under many names, of which the most familiar to nonspecialists would be the variations on the term *bwete.* It was the paramount traditional cult of the Tsogho, among whom it developed into a ritual and theatrical complex. The name was appropriated by a more recent Tsogho offshoot of *bwete,* the syncretistic

Bwiti religion, which, to all appearances, did not continue the focus on relics.

Not all of the analogous cults were known under cognates of the term *bwete*. The practice was known as *alumbi* in parts of now westcentral and southwest Gabon. On the now southern Cameroun coast and for some distance inland, the designation *melan* prevailed. Special details of rationale and ritual proliferated locally as the idea spread through the wider region.

Some of the bones of important relatives ultimately served as contact points with nature spirits. They were equally important in imbuing certain substances with their power. The white clay and the barwood powder kept in the reliquary would then enter into medicines, signs of status, and personally owned reliquaries.

The relics were kept in different kinds of containers, according either to region and ethnic group or to the cult that used them. Some societies—the Mbete, Mbamba, and, seemingly, the Sango—had several discrete relic-based cults, not all of which were defined by family membership (cat. no. 30).

Among those peoples greatly concerned with trade and wealth, a lack of success was attributed to supernatural interference with the power of the relics used by the cult. At some point in its inception the cult apparently anticipated this weakness by including the reliquary guardian figure in its system. Conceived in diverse shapes (cat. nos. 29–34, 36, 38) and invested with a supernatural power not yet fully understood, these figures surmounted reliquaries in order to ward off intruders, human or other.

The brass adornment of the guardian often evoked the idea of daylight—evil was believed to be stronger at night—and its pose in the more naturalistic images may have alluded to the detection and defeat of intruders. This variability in representation might suggest that, once established, the guardian figure began to develop culturally on its own terms, following aesthetic premises and leadership incentives into a field where the images replicated the concern of their makers with personal beauty and supernatural power.

The Ngumba, who disseminated the cult to some of their neighbors, began to mount several guardian figures on the same reliquary.[11] Other followers of the western version of the cult assembled their guardian figures at times of crisis, to introduce them to the newly initiated and to entertain themselves by manipulating the statues in theatrical performances.

In the eastern version of the cult, the Hongwe and Shamaye began to make simpler, smaller, and conceivably "junior" images to coexist with the more important ones.[12] Guardian figures were individualized and given their own special powers and their own names, not those of the deceased whose bones they guarded. These aspects of inventiveness and play—and perhaps redundance—may have contributed to the occasional willingness of cult members to take guardian figures out of their traditional context, in order to sell them, upon request, to Europeans. (Series of excellent figures in the same carvers' styles, and showing very little wear, strongly suggest that these carvers—and brass workers—were working for both their cult members and Europeans.) The cult's relics, however, were inalienable.

MASKING

Masking—the other major aspect of iconography in this region—demonstrates an equally strong belief in tutelary spirits summoned from nature. The almost unbroken distribution and intensive use of disguise in this connection demonstrates the great diversity of form and behavior that this

40 SIDE PANELS OF AN
ALTAR FRAME
Tsogho or Pove (Vuvi); central
Gabon; 20th century
Wood and pigment
67 x 5 in. (170 x 12.5 cm)

These stelalike uprights represent a two-dimensional mode in the large-scale furnishing of the main cult house. They were erected for important rites in the temple and at secluded outdoor sites. Set upright in the ground, they formed the sides of a prosceniumlike frame spanned by an often deep lintel decorated with geometric and representational forms. These elements framed important sacred objects of the cult, such as portable altars and a boxed representation of a mythical ancestor. The figural themes on the side panels represent the primal couple and very often are asymmetrical in their decoration. All of the frame was kept hidden when not in use. The style of the heads in these particular Tsogho panels is very close to that ascribed to the neighboring Pove people.

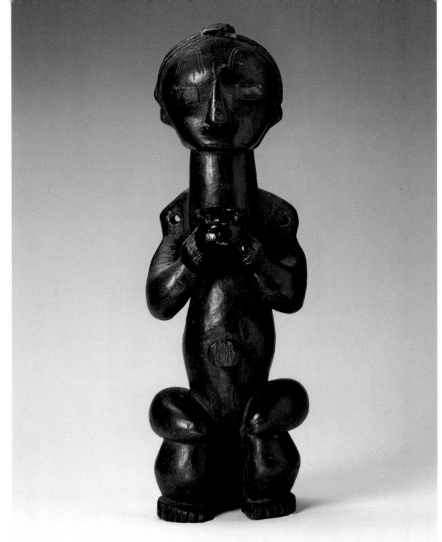

belief allowed. Indeed, in the Eastern Ivindo River basin (among peoples not represented in the Strong Collection) some kinds of masks could attain a level of cultural importance that led to their use as reliquary guardians.

In its animated persona the mask played roles that enabled cults to deal in many and particular ways with the crises that beset traditional life. Patterns of masking were in great part expressions of cultural idiosyncrasy. Reading from the woefully sparse documentation of performances, no strong regional consistencies are found. Thus, whereas the Mbete and, probably, the Mbamba brought out maskers (cat. nos. 18–20) to celebrate the birth of twins, the Kwele, who also welcomed twins, did not observe this convention. Instead, they used their masks primarily to strengthen belief in the efficacy of a medicine, the preparation of which brought disaffected village segments together in times of crisis.[13]

Denise Paulme's oft-cited aphorism, "The form travels alone, free of all meaning,"[14] came to us through her discussion of the uses of masks in this region. Although somewhat overstated, it directs attention to the shifts in form and function undergone by mask types as they spread from one society to another.

The Strong Collection makes an important case for the play of particularity in the traditional art of a region. Its holdings, mostly selected contrary to art-collecting fashion, indicate much wider horizons than would be found convenient by the popularizing milieu of African art. An ethnologically grounded consideration of the submerged and particular aspects of two styles that are significantly represented in the collection—Fang and Kwele—is presented below.

Fang

This statuary style, most admired by Western connoisseurs, may, in specialist perspective, include at least three distinct styles attributable to peoples who were culturally separate from the Fang. These would be the Ngumba, including the Mabea, whose origin, language, and history are different from those of the Fang; certain coastal peoples of the Bube-Benga group; and the Fang's northern relatives who deny being Fang and differ from them culturally to a significant degree.

Early French explorers and the colonial writers and administrators to follow subscribed to the notion that the power in numbers and forcefulness of the incoming Fang was equivalent to cultural superiority. This premise developed into a scenario in which the Fang taught their new neighbors ideas and techniques—including the cult of relics and the use of guardian figures—that virtually transformed them into would-be Fang while they continued to observe their traditional identity. This dynamic of presumed influence was thought of as *pahouinisation,* or, in my translation, "Fang(u)ization."

Contemporaneous American writers in Africa did not share this view. From 1861 onward they regarded the Fang material culture as less sophisticated (in all but metalwork) than those of the longer-settled peoples. Fang modes of coiffure and personal adornment were much simpler than those that later distinguished their statues.[15] The relic cult and its use of statuary flourished among non-Fang peoples on the coast while the Fang were coming south.[16] Moreover, the northern and western relatives of the Fang admitted to having received their version of the cult from the Ngumba, who had been in contact with the coast considerably longer.[17]

It seems likely that Fang power led some non-Fang groups to seeing the advantage of becoming Fang. Such opportunistic transformations were common throughout the region well before the advent of the Fang and continued among other peoples well after. All told, Fang influence on other traditional cultures appears to have been much more demographic than cultural. Analysis of Fang patterns of lending and borrowing cultural elements in relation to longer settled societies has come due.

The premise of premigration Fang culture being the same as that recorded by Europeans during the nineteenth century bears importantly on the history of their art. Failure to question particulars of history and ethnicity has resulted in a grab bag of unexplained discrete styles. The identities of these traditions depend on the further investigation of interrelationship on the level of localities and artists.

One aspect of the Fang migration brings out its legacy of complexity in the development of statuary style. When the Fang pushed through the present southern Cameroun they encountered a large group of Ngumba (in the broad sense) who may already have begun to move southward, either as a reaction to the anticipated pressure of the Fang mass or on their own initiative in search of trade advantages. They often proceeded alongside—but apart from—the Fang.

No direct evidence is available of Fang statuary style during this migratory period. The essential differences between Ngumba and Fang material culture in the nineteenth century never came to be adequately noted in published form. Some records might imply that an Ngumba tradition of guardian statuary was extant at the beginning of the nineteenth century,[18] thus antedating the main surge of the Fang into the northwestern Ogowe River basin. Events in the southward movement may have worked changes in Ngumba style, perhaps through accommodation to the sculptural styles of the relic cults of the owners of the land they acquired. Success in trade of such predecessors may have indicated that the local imagery worked best with the local nature spirits.

Percolating from the days of early colonial administration down through the current art market, the notion of *pahouinisation* has condensed a multifarious and dynamic history of change into a simple tale of conquest and subsequent culture lending. It should have long since evoked some curiosity as to its begging questions of the homogeneity of the Fang people through the nineteenth century and the perpetuity of their original culture.

29 SEATED FEMALE FIGURE HOLDING A VESSEL
Fang, probably a westcentral group; central and southwestern Equatorial Guinea and adjacent Gabon; ca. 1900
Wood, pigment, oil, and metal
15½ x 5 in. (39.5 x 12.5 cm)

The greatest differences in traditional reliquary guardian style seem to prevail in examples from Rio Muni, Equatorial Guinea. The cup-bearing theme appears most frequently in the sector cited for this example. So far, it has been explained as either a warning gesture based on a poison ordeal or a supplication for some kinds of offerings.

The mystique of the name "Fang" exerts a gravitational pull on non-Fang images whose styles are somewhat similar and yet conceivably seminal to the monuments of that art. The financial repute of Fang statuary has by now spread to any object that can be called Fang, and many are so called. Indeed, sometimes similarity need not matter greatly.

For example, a half-figure mainly in Tsogho style, central Gabon, proved perplexing in that its flexed arms were joined in front of its body in a pose characteristic of Fang iconography. X-ray photographs revealed that later the arms had been carved separately and joined to the figure, the finish of which was the lustrous dark color—in this case black—associated with Fang guardian statues. In another instance, a Tsogho mask bearing some resemblance to Fang style is documented as coming from a Tsogho village; still, it works its way through the art market as a Fang mask. And a typical Senufo figure from the Ivory Coast of a mother on a stool, holding an infant, has its face altered enough to allow its public sale as a Fang rarity.

Kwele

The Strong Collection is fortunate in its inclusion of five masks from the Kwele people and groups related to them by descent or culture (cat. nos. 11–15). Through a combination of the carvers' remarkable imagination and technique, the dealers' astute merchandising, and a favorable obscurity of background, Kwele masks became highly desirable as soon as they appeared on the market in limited numbers through the 1950s. Their appeal quickly raised prices. These commercial aspects occasioned the accretion of a mystique of Kwele traditional art, a kind of European-imposed mythology that should be addressed before it is too late.

Quite expectably, here the same pull of gravity operates as in the case of Fang art. Any work that a subjective view finds similar to works already attributed to the Kwele will itself assume a Kwele origin. This "Kwele" rubric takes in works of the Njem and Yesa, who, with the possible exception of the contemporary Yesa and their relatives, cannot be considered as Kwele. Whereas these peoples do live in the wider region that includes the Kwele, a fair number of works ascribed to the Kwele seem to fall outside of that region.

Here, too, my point in dealing with the Kwele is to forestall the assimilation of sales talk into ethnology and art history. In this case, ethnic identity, traditionality, and artistic quality have suffered distortion and limitation in order to maintain commercial standards. Since the late 1940s, the presence of Kwele masks and the lack of detailed and disinterested information about them has evolved into a wishful fantasy working together colonial adventures, irresponsible deductions from popular ethnology, and arbitrary, yet absolutely stated, judgments on authenticity and artistic quality. Short outlines of traditional masking among the Kwele have appeared,[19] but they have not addressed the Western consensus on the matter. The following outline again takes up the subject but focuses on details that the market need not have overlooked or suppressed.

In 1960–61 I spent fifteen months among the Kwele of the then Brazzaville-Congo nation (now the People's Republic of the Congo) and the Gabon, but, especially among the former, where the carving of masks had flourished. My research concern, directed toward a doctoral dissertation,[20] was with the presence and use of masks among the precolonial Kwele. I approached the subject as an anthropologist; that is, I endeavored to understand the phenomenon against the background of the whole culture. My research time was allocated more to cultural subsystems than to masks alone. The extent of my inquiries may furnish some perspective on the Western notions of Kwele traditional culture.

The Kwele say that they lived at the headwaters of the Ivindo River at the beginning of the nineteenth century. They seem to have been the southeasternmost members of the Makaa-Njem language group. They were then unacquainted with the major religious system that later distinguished their culture. If they had masks, they did not use them systematically.

In troubled times, the Kwele managed to hold their own against their neighbors. Yet circumstances led to their migrating south and east. After a decade or two in their new lands while living and trading with their Ngom- and Kota-related neighbors, they built up their numbers and wealth.

Kwele culture of those days was characterized by the great mobility and autonomy of minor lineage groups. Clan segments in search of wealth and power would move into villages composed of many other unrelated clan segments. The large, fortified villages of those troubled times had only two kinds of building: guardhouse (or men's house) and dwelling house.

The regulation of village and extravillage affairs depended, in principle, on the consensus of the heads of the resident lineages. The prevailing opportunism of these times, however, often resulted in failure to reach consensus. Villages tended to split apart, their components going off to join other villages or to found new ones. Kwele leaders tried to counteract this divisiveness by magical means.

Their most important allies in the period of regrouping were the Yesa ("Ngwyes" in Kwele), an Ngom-related people. At about the middle of the nineteenth century, when a smallpox epidemic swept through the region, the Kwele obtained a powerful "medicine," *byet,* from the Yesa. "Medicine" in this sense meant a complex ritual procedure, which involved powerful family relics, divination by hunting, the visits of nature spirits represented by maskers and disguised voices, the administering of a panacea, and a final rite of expiation and purification.

The apparent success of *byet* (*beete* in Kwele) in uniting the village led to its continual performance and elaboration by the Kwele using it to deal with all major crises. The cult quickly diffused throughout the Kwele population.

As the "children of *beete,*" maskers represented spirits of the forest, usually showing animal and plant attributes, even though their faces tended to be human. Nothing is known of the mask forms that the Yesa transmitted with *beete* to the Kwele; that the borrowers elaborated on type and style, however, seems very likely.

Beete masks existed primarily to dance. They were made to enliven occasions with their beauty, movements, and suggestion of power. Maskers came out mainly to divert the populace during the sometimes lengthy preparation

11 HELMET MASK
Njem; People's Republic of the Congo and southeastern Cameroun; 20th century
Wood and pigment
15½ x 10½ in. (39.5 x 26.5 cm)

This mask type is believed to have been borrowed from the Kwele, but it combines the morphology of one type with the persona of another. It served mainly to menace and extort.

of the *beete* panacea. One after another, they led the villagers in dancing through the days. The ritual cycle included the initiation of youths into the secrets of the cult; these candidates were then introduced to the skulls of important deceased leaders and to the detached (or inactive) masks. Only masks that danced were shown; no frontal masks were used for ritual purposes other than dancing.

In certain localities *beete* candidates, before their introduction to the masks, would be put into a palisaded enclosure containing a small house from which maskers would emerge to haze them. This small house was provisional, built only for that moment in the cycle and not for use as a cult house.[21]

Cult houses were not part of Kwele traditional culture; the village had no room for them, and the lineages that owned cult materials would not risk their loss by keeping them in a building outside of the village. The only cult site that *beete* had was an isolated glade in the forest where carvers worked, dancers and musicians practiced, and maskers were disguised before appearing in public.

Beete paraphernalia belonged to lineages, not to the cult itself; but not all lineages owned masks. When *beete* leaders needed masks to appear, they asked their owners to bring them in on loan. Villages often borrowed masks from other villages. Otherwise, lineage leaders kept their masks hidden, either in their guard houses or in forbidden chambers in their dwelling houses. The Kwele had no exclusive building in which to hang their masks when not in use.

Beete remained one of the central institutions of Kwele culture into the first decades of the twentieth century, serving the needs of a society subject to many and diverse crises. When it proved ineffectual against colonial military power—French and German—the ever-pragmatic Kwele abandoned it. Most of the cult materials were simply allowed to decay, or indigenous witch-hunting movements forced their destruction. The mask most important to *beete,* a simple palm leaf carapace, somehow retained its power into the 1960s.

Ritual masking using wooden types waned before the 1920s. Some nostalgic lineages commissioned a few for their own entertainment. Probably no more than ten masks from the *beete* era came to France in the early 1910s. The apparent absence of Kwele masks in German museums is surprising, in view of the fact that Germany held the most mask-prolific Kwele sector through much of the 1910s.

In the late 1920s colonial administrators in French Equatorial Africa grew aware of the rising value of African traditional sculpture on the Paris market. Those who saw a few masks among the Kwele commissioned more from the same men who had carved masks for *beete* in its heyday. Both cash incentive and love of carving motivated these artists, many of whom were young men when they took up their calling. At least two excellent carvers were still working when I was among the eastern Kwele in the early 1960s.

The lure of cash also encouraged the growth in the 1930s of a school of Kwele *débrouillards,* resourceful young men with no previous training who strove to work things out on their own by improvising on models seen in the workplaces of the masters. From what I saw and was told, these amateur-made masks were carved in innocence, with no intent to deceive and no knowledge of what would appeal to Europeans. This cottage industry in traditional mask types produced many examples that went from subprefecture to prefecture to Brazzaville and Pointe-Noire, tributaries flowing into rivers flowing into the sea.

These colonial masks came to Paris in the mid- and late 1930s. Some found their place in the then Musée d'Outre-Mer. Others came up on the market, where they were greatly admired and quickly sold. Their unusual style and remarkable quality allayed all doubt about their authenticity. Moreover, in those years there were fewer collectors, and they were concerned more with intrinsic form than with any validating dossier of ceremonial use.

Some carvers adhered to their precolonial training and made masks as if they would be worn in the dance, furnishing them with holes at the top and sides for the cords that would secure them to their wearers' heads. Other carvers, no less accomplished, knew that Europeans wanted the masks for souvenirs and decorative effects; they spared themselves the trouble of burning through the harness holes. Some solid masklike objects had a face on either side, a complete departure from tradition.

In the following decades, as the general African art market vastly increased, anxiety over too fulsome a supply led to the dogmatic equation of authenticity with "tribal ritual use." This watchword expressed a romantic assurance that an artist trained in a traditional, technologically simple society could not produce affecting imagery without total faith in his local religion.

Yet the example of Kwele masks seems to refute this premise. Traditional Kwele carvers working beyond the end of their religious tradition produced masks rightly considered to be masterpieces of both Kwele and African art. The absence of an adequate corpus of precolonial masks prevents the assumption that later works were in any way inferior. Indeed, according to the specific details of the carvers' lives and their freedom from traditional strictures, some may have done their best work after the fact. This exception would apply only to the carvers who had begun their careers before the twilight of *beete.* One would not expect the carvers and carpenters in following generations to excel in a tradition they had never learned. This is not to say, however, that all or most carvers excelled—according to Western standards—in traditional times.

Whether of internal or external origin, most copies run counter to the Kwele masters' rationale. Traditional Kwele carvers understood that their masks represented spirits as personae and varied the features to make this apparent. The facsimiles that dealers and auction galleries fail to screen out of their stock often originate in the workshops of non-Kwele ethnic groups, often in other parts of Africa.

Lately dealers have become stuck to the tar baby that grew out of their "authenticity equals ritual use" formula. Collectors and scholars have begun to remark on the absence of harness holes and signs of wear on the great masks of this genre. Rather than leave the question open, some sellers have invented a scenario suggesting that the traditional Kwele danced about thrusting some of their masks outward at their sides, manipulating them as if operating a steering wheel. The dignity of the art is thus sacrificed, perhaps for posterity, for the extrinsic value of the object.

NOTES

1. I use the term "Kwele" only to conform with the convention of suppressing Bantu plural prefixes in published discourse. The contraction would probably be meaningless to the Bakwele themselves.

2. Reference to certain language speakers designates members of the language groups or clusters of this region defined by Malcolm Guthrie in *The Bantu Languages of Western Equatorial Africa* (London: International African Institute, 1953). This scheme brings together ethnic groups according to their use of closely related languages. It can serve to imply primal historical and, to a lesser extent, cultural relationships between the art-producing peoples represented in the Strong Collection and to provide an economical way of designating them collectively.

Group	Languages
Bube-Benga	Benga: southern coast of Equatorial Guinea and adjacent Gabon.
Basa	Mbene and BaKogo (Koko of some authors): north, northeast, and south of Douala.
Yaunde-Fang	Ewondo: southwest of Yaounde in Cameroun. Bulu: southwestern Cameroun. Fang: southwestern Cameroun; almost all of inland Equatorial Guinea; northwestern to central Gabon.
Makaa-Njem	Ngumba: southwestern Cameroun, northwestern Equatorial Guinea. Njem: southeastern Cameroun and adjacent People's Republic of the Congo. Kwele: continuous through southern Ngoko River basin of People's Republic of the Congo and northeast Ivindo River basin of Gabon and People's Republic of the Congo.
Kele	Kele (called Ngom here): widely dispersed through central and eastcentral Gabon and westcentral People's Republic of the Congo. Shekiani: coast of northwest Gabon. Bubi (possibly Pove or "Vuvi"): central Gabon, west of Koulamoutou. Wumbu: southcentral Gabon and eastcentral People's Republic of the Congo. Kota (including Hongwe, Shamaye, Ndasa, and true Kota): Gabon, Upper Eastern Ivindo River basin, Upper Ogowe River basin; People's Republic of the Congo, Upper Ogowe and Upper Kouilou River basins.
Myene	Mpongwe: Gabon estuary region. Galwa: westcentral Gabon, region of Lambaréné.
Tsogho	Tsogho: central Gabon. Kande: central Gabon, region of Booué.
Shira-Punu	Punu: southwest Gabon and adjacent People's Republic of the Congo. Sangu (Shango, Sango): northern group in central Gabon; southern group in southwest Gabon.
Njabi	Nzebi: central Gabon and adjacent People's Republic of the Congo.
Mbete	Mbete: eastcentral Gabon and adjacent People's Republic of the Congo. Mbamba: southeastern Gabon; southcentral People's Republic of the Congo. Ndumu: southeastern Gabon, region of Franceville.

3. Paul B. Du Chaillu, an American trader, explored extensively in the region that now takes in southern Equatorial Guinea and westcentral and central Gabon. Through the 1850s and 1860s he came to know many of the peoples whose art we now study, and he provided valuable ethnographic observations of the region before the full force of the Fang migration and the direct influence of the European presence. Paul B. Du Chaillu, *Explorations and Adventures in Equatorial Africa* (New York: Harper, 1861), 59–79, 90, 187–198.

4. Jean-Louis Paudrat, "From Africa," in *"Primitivism" in Twentieth Century Art: Affinity of the Tribal and the Modern,* ed. William Rubin (New York: The Museum of Modern Art, 1984), 1:124–175.

5. Louis Perrois, *La statuaire fang Gabon* (Paris: ORSTOM, 1972).

6. James W. Fernandez and Renate Fernandez, "Fang Reliquary Art: Its Quantities and Qualities," *Cahiers d'études africaines* 15, no. 4 (1975): 723–746.

7. Alain Chaffin and Françoise Chaffin, *L'art kota* (Meudon: Chaffin, 1979).

8. Günter Tessmann, *Die Pangwe: Völkerkundliche Monographie eines westafrikanischen Negerstammes,* 2 vols. (Berlin: Ernst Wasmuth, 1913), 1, 59, Abb. 19; 1, 244–251, Abb. 196–203.

9. Otto Gollnhofer, Pierre Sallée, and Roger Sillans, *Art et artisanat tsogho* (Paris: ORSTOM, 1975), 35–49.

10. Leon Siroto, *African Spirit Images and Identities* (New York: Pace Primitive Art, 1976), 6–22, 102.

11. Eckart von Sydow, *Afrikanische Plastik* (New York: George Wittenborn, Inc., 1954), pl. 51B; Kurt Krieger, *Westafrikanische Plastik* (Berlin: Museum für Völkerkunde, 1965), 1:82.

12. Louis Perrois, *Arts du Gabon: les Arts plastiques du bassin de l'Ogooué* (Paris: ORSTOM; Arnouville: Arts d'Afrique noire, 1979), 149, 241–291.

13. Leon Siroto, "Witchcraft Belief in the Explanation of Traditional African Iconography," in *The Visual Arts: Plastic and Graphic,* ed. Justine M. Cordwell (The Hague: Mouton, 1979), 254–255.

14. My translation; see Denise Paulme, *La sculpture de l'Afrique noire* (Paris: Presses Universitaires de France, 1956), 90.

15. Du Chaillu, *Explorations,* 92–93, 95.

16. John Leighton Wilson, *Western Africa* (New York: Harper, 1856), 393–394; R. H. Nassau, *Fetishism in West Africa* (New York: Scribners, 1904), 159, 320, 326.

17. Philippe Laburthe-Tolra, *Initiations et sociétés secrètes au Cameroun* (Paris: Editions Karthala, 1985), 337.

18. Laburthe-Tolra, *Initiations,* 337.

19. Siroto, "Witchcraft," 254–260; Leon Siroto, "Gon: A Mask Used in Competition for Leadership among the BaKwele," in *African Art and Leadership,* eds. Douglas Fraser and Herbert M. Cole (Madison: University of Wisconsin Press, 1972), 57–77.

20. Leon Siroto, *Masks and Social Organization among the BaKwele People of Western Equatorial Africa* (Ann Arbor, Mich.: University Microfilms, 1970).

21. William Fagg, *Masques d'Afrique* (Paris: Editions Fernand Nathan, 1980), 114; Louis Perrois, *Ancestral Art of Gabon from the Collections of the Barbier-Mueller Museum,* exh. cat. (Geneva: Musée Barbier-Mueller, 1985), 58.

CATALOGUE OF OBJECTS

Leon Siroto

NOTE TO THE CAPTIONS:

Dimensions are given in both inches and centimeters, height preceding width.

Pieces in the Dwight and Blossom Strong Collection were generally collected in Africa during two time periods: the turn of the century (1880–1920) and the decades immediately following (1920–1950). Precise dates are not possible for most objects. In these captions, objects designated as 20th century date between 1920 and 1950.

Masks and Headdresses

1 HELMET MASK WITH
INSERTED HORNLIKE FORMS
Fang or Bulu; southcentral Cameroun
and adjacent Gabon; 20th century
Wood, pigment, fiber, and resin
19½ x 15 in. (with horns)
(49.5 x 37 cm)

This mask's style, distinguished by
its heart-shaped face, agrees with
that of masks collected near the
Gabon/Cameroun border in the
1900s. The model for this type of
mask would ultimately have been a
helmet mask with winglike crests,
all carved from one piece of wood by
the Ngom and their relatives, who
doubtless preceded the Fang in this
region and who regarded this mask as
the most important in their considerable inventory. Subsequently, the
Fang were less impressed by the religious aspect of the mask; they saved
time by carving the "horns" separately and then securing them into
the crown of the mask, in this case,
by a mortise-and-tenon joint, skill-
fully concealed by an overlay of a
resinlike substance. A fair number of
masks of this general type were
found widely among the Fang. Their
use was probably festive in a nonreli-
gious sense.

2 Four-faced helmet mask
Fang; probably across northern
Equatorial Guinea and Gabon;
20th century
Wood, pigment, fiber, and accretions
10 x 12¼ in. (25.5 x 31 cm)

The *ngontangan* mask type probably originated near the juncture of northern Equatorial Guinea, northern Gabon, and southwestern Cameroun. It appears to have been a synthesis of mask styles and dance movements already established in the region. Its Fang name, meaning "the young white woman," reflects the belief in supernatural power inherent in the European and American missionaries, especially among the women, who were very rare on the coast in the nineteenth century. The mask's miniature aspect is challenging, in view of its heavily used condition. A pad on the inside of the crown suggests that the mask was adjusted to fit different wearers.

3 Face mask
Fang; northwestern to westcentral
Gabon, Equatorial Guinea,
and southcentral Cameroun;
early 20th century
Wood, pigment, and fiber
10 (mask only) x 7 in. (25.5 x 18 cm)

The style and format here suggest the retention for further use, perhaps by children, as part of an *ngontangan* mask. A few other known examples show the same qualities. The simple facial features, the lack of a mouth, and the ornamental marking (representing tattoo patterns) may indicate one of the earliest styles in which these masks were carved.

4 FOUR-FACED HELMET MASK
Fang; probably northern Equatorial
Guinea; 20th century
Wood, pigment, fiber,
feathers, and resin
20 (mask only) x 13¼ in.
(51 x 33.5 cm)

This mask, showing clear evidence of
use in the dance, may represent one
of the furthest extents of improvisation on decoration in *ngontangan*
style. The customary use of dark
color has been reversed, thus giving
the impression of a negative transfor-
mation, with white prevailing in the
general scheme. The relatively naturalistic faces with high-bridged noses
are characteristic of more recent Fang
mask styles in Rio Muni.

5 BIFRONTAL HELMET MASK
Fang or Bulu; northwestern
Gabon/southwestern Cameroun;
20th century
Wood, pigment, and fiber
ca. 13¼ (mask only) x 9 in.
(33.5 x 23 cm)

Bifrontal helmet masks are obviously
related in form to the four-faced kind
but are not necessarily associated
with the same rationale, performance,
and name *(ngontangan)*. In Equatorial
Guinea the proliferation of masking
has led to a casual attitude toward
terminology; any white-faced mask
is *ngontangan*. As yet, no information
exists on the roles played by Fang
bifrontal masks.

6 FACE MASK
Fang; northwestern Gabon, probably
basins of the Como and Abanga
Rivers; early 20th century
Wood, pigment, and fiber
10½ (mask only) x 6 in.
(26.5 x 15 cm)

The small size of this mask calls to
mind a watercolor by the Swiss missionary F. Grébert in the collection
of the Barbier-Mueller Museum,
Geneva, showing a similar mask
worn by a stilt dancer between
parallel ranks of youths.

7 FACE MASK
Fang; northwestern Gabon, probably
basins of the Como and Abanga
Rivers; 20th century
Wood and pigment
16 x 8 in. (40.5 x 20.5 cm)

The use of this type of mask is
unknown. On the strength of one
laconic attribution of a narrow,
white-faced mask from the *ngii* cult
among the Fang, all masks showing
these features have come to be attributed to the same cult. As very little
information exists on the traditional
use of masks among the Fang, this
could be a flagrant oversimplifica-
tion. Perhaps it would be more
enlightened to think of uses, rather
than a one-to-one relationship
between form and use.

8 FACE MASK WITH ARTICU-
LATED LOWER JAW
An undetermined people; central
Gabon or possibly the coast of
Equatorial Guinea; 20th century
Wood, pigment, rubber, and metal
12 x 11 in. (30.5 x 28 cm)

This seemingly unique mask was
acquired in the understanding that it
came from Rio Muni, the mainland
part of Equatorial Guinea, which the
Fang occupy. Only the simplified features, whitened surface, and flush
eye-holes of this mask suggest Fang
mask style, which varies greatly. The
basic form—exclusive of the inflated
cheeks—leads to the consideration
that its origin was central Gabon.
The backward tilt of the nose and
inner cheeks and especially the
graceful curve of the eyebrows com-
pare well with Tsogho style. The
original main cult of the Tsogho had
a theater of masks employing an
extensive roster of personae, some of
which distinguished themselves by
trick effects. A European rubber band
determines the movement of the
mask's jaw.

9 DANCE HEADDRESS
Saa (Basa), Mbene group;
southwestern Cameroun; ca. 1900
Wood, pigment, and fiber
24¼ x 5¼ in. (61.5 x 13.5 cm)

This headdress was part of a disguise
worn by dancers of a men's cult in
the representation of women.

10 HEADDRESS (?)
Saa (Basa), Mbene group; southwestern Cameroun; 20th century
Wood, pigment, and hair
19¼ x 4¾ in. (49 x 12 cm)

Comparison with the preceding indicates a fantasist's departure within the same style and iconography. Note especially the characteristic coiffure. This carver, perhaps the founder of a short-lived school, produced a number of comparable works, all markedly different from each other. Whether those were used as headdresses is unknown.

11 HELMET MASK
See page 19.

12 FACE MASK WITH TUSKS
Kwele, eastern group; People's Republic of the Congo; 20th century
Wood and pigment
15¼ x 8 in. (38.5 x 20.5 cm)

The classic "fierce" mask took the form of a gorilla's skull. Its popularity led to experimentation with form, often resulting in more anthropomorphic types. This mask might be the work of the master carver Abanda of Aadyaala village.

13 FACE MASK REPRESENTING A SWALLOW

Kwele, eastern group; People's Republic of the Congo; 20th century
Wood, pigment, and metal
14¼ x 10¼ in. (36 x 26 cm)

The Kwele greatly admired the swallow for its grace in flight and its lustrous plumage and, perhaps, for its absence during part of each year. Examples of such masks by at least four carvers are extant.

14 FACE MASK

Kwele, eastern group; People's Republic of the Congo; 20th century
Wood and pigment
12¼ x 11½ in. (31 x 29 cm)

This wide, "beautiful" mask was one of two types expected to dance in the women's style. It could thus perform with male mask types that otherwise would have danced alone. The carver of this mask, Abanda of Aadyaala village, was elderly in 1961; in his youth he carved for the *beete* cult.

15 FOUR-FACED HELMET MASK
Yesa (Ngwyes); northwestern
People's Republic of the Congo
and northeastern Gabon: basin of
the Djouah River; 20th century
Wood and pigment
17½ x 9½ in. (44.5 x 24 cm)

The Yesa are a Kele-speaking population who have been assimilating into
the Kwele since the early part of this
century. Both they and the Kwele
borrowed the *ngontangan* mask from
the Fang and the Bulu, and dropped
its ritual significance.

16 FACE MASK
A people of the Myene group,
Galwa or Mpongwe; coast of northern
and central Gabon; 20th century
Wood, pigment, and iron
11½ x 7½ in. (29 x 19 cm)

Myene society entrusted cult members wearing this type of mask with
a considerable degree of authority
in the regulation of a community's
behavior. The masker could restrict
parts of the forest in the interest of
conserving vital resources. As in
many other West African societies,
he emerged in times of crisis to warn
and chastise wayward villagers. The
survival of this mask and its retention of power are remarkable in the
context of Myene commercial activity and strong secular government.

17 FACE MASK

Kande; central Gabon, region of
Booué on the Middle Ogowe River;
20th century
Wood, pigment, fiber, iron,
and feathers
10 (mask only) x 6¼ in. (25.5 x 16 cm)

The Kande were renowned canoe-
men, intensely involved with the
river trade through the nineteenth
century, toward the end of which
their numbers began to wane dramat-
ically. They are Tsogho speakers, but
their art seems to incline in style and
use toward those of other peoples on
the Ogowe River. A masker wearing
a disguise similar to this example
appears in a film taken in the Kande
village of Kongo Boumba in 1946.

18 FACE MASK

Mbete or Mbamba; southeastern
Gabon/central-to-southwestern
People's Republic of the Congo;
20th century
Wood and pigment
13 x 8 in. (33 x 20.5 cm)

The Mbamba and Mbete are closely
related in language and culture. Their
masks, invariably frontal, may differ
in style, but collection data have not
yet made this clear. Both styles show
a reductive, cubistic approach to the
human face, and both adhere to the
common principle of red-and-white
pigmentation in sizable contrastive
blocks.

19 FACE MASK
Mbete or Mbamba; southeastern
Gabon/central-to-southwestern
People's Republic of the Congo;
20th century
Wood and pigment
14½ x 5 in. (37 x 12.5 cm)

See text of cat. no. 18.

20 FACE MASK
Mbete or Mbamba; southeastern
Gabon/central-to-southwestern
People's Republic of the Congo;
20th century
Wood and pigment
19¼ x 8 in. (49 x 20.5 cm)

See text of cat. no. 18.

21 FACE MASK
Nzebi and northern Sango style elements; central Gabon; 20th century
Wood and pigment
13¼ x 7¼ in. (33.5 x 18.5 cm)

The convexity of brow, nose, and face probably reflect a Nzebi canon. Playing off against the relatively long, narrow face, these features strongly suggest an accommodation to northern Sango style. The whitened depressions under the eyes may symbolize clairvoyance. The quartering of masks and faces by blocks of contrasting color extends from central Gabon to southern Cameroun but seems not to be universal either through the region or within any ethnic group. The larger holes at the edge of the mask below the level of the mouth indicate the presence of a bit which, clenched between the wearer's teeth, kept the mask in place during acrobatic feats.

22 FACE MASK
Possibly Nzebi or northern Sango; central Gabon; 20th century
Wood, pigment, and fiber
13 x 6¾ in. (33 x 17 cm)

The high-bridged nose, in contrast to the usually flat noses of other ethnic styles making up the regional complex, often serves as a diagnostic feature of Nzebi masks.

23 FACE MASK
Northern Sango; central Gabon;
20th century
Wood, pigment, and fiber
14¼ x 8 in. (36 x 20.5 cm)

These long, relatively flat masks
with ornate and highly arched eyebrows are believed to have been
ritually equivalent to the masks in
the Shira-Punu style used by the
southern Sango—although they do
not perform on stilts. Some examples
of this style seem to represent a tran-
sition between the Shira-Punu and
central Gabon complex mask styles.
The cane-strip bit across the lower
back of this mask suggests that the
wearer's dance involved acrobatic
movements.

24 FACE MASK

Northern Sango; central Gabon;
20th century
Wood, pigment, fiber, and iron
10¼ x 7½ in. (26 x 19 cm)

The arching tiaralike form across
the top of the mask is characteristic
of this style. The vertical band of
pigment on the chin may allude to
the wearing, below the mask, of the
pelt of a genet—a small, lithe carni-
vore often symbolically associated
with the dance in this region. The
nails around the sides of the face
served to secure a heavy mane of
shredded raffia.

25 FACE MASK

Shira-Punu, probably Lumbu; southwestern Gabon and southwestern
People's Republic of the Congo;
20th century
Wood, pigment, fiber, and metal
8¾ x 8½ in. (22 x 21.5 cm)

This much-used mask shows a coiffure that French experts regard as
closely associated with the Lumbu.
It differs considerably from the crest-
and-side-locks format that distin-
guishes most examples of Shira-Punu
mask style. Here instead are a series
of pendant braids on either side of the
midline of the head. This hairstyle
does not appear in the longer-known
examples of Shira-Punu art and may
have come into the corpus later in
this century.

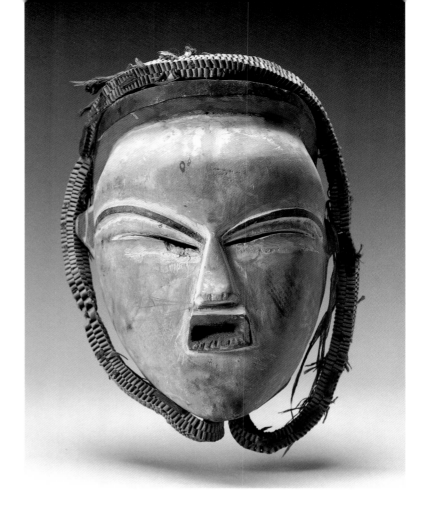

26 FACE MASK
Tsogho; central Gabon; 20th century
Wood, pigment, fiber, and metal
11½ x 8¼ in. (29 x 21 cm)

This mask embodies the most characteristic Tsogho sculptural style, seemingly not shared by contiguous but unrelated ethnic groups. Masks of many styles, formal types, and personae performed in public and secret ceremonies of the main Tsogho cult.

Reliquaries and Figures

27 SEATED MALE FIGURE
Probably Ngumba; southwestern Cameroun and coastal inland of Equatorial Guinea; 20th century
Wood, pigment, metal, fiber, and feathers
11½ (figure only) x 4 in. (29 x 10 cm)

This reliquary guardian for the *melan* cult shows an unusual treatment of the face, perhaps distinctive enough to suggest the influence of another style. The traditional sculpture of the coastal peoples of southern Cameroun and Equatorial Guinea remains to be studied.

28 CROUCHING MALE FIGURE HOLDING A BOXLIKE OBJECT

Fang, probably a westcentral group or Ngumba; Equatorial Guinea; 20th century
Wood, pigment, metal, and feathers
10 (figure only) x 3¼ in.
(25.5 x 8.5 cm)

Strong Ngumba influence is apparent in this statue, especially in the lower trunk and the legs. The abundant presence of brass evokes the idea of daylight and, in turn, the deflection of harmful power. The feather crown was primarily for a martial effect and thus appropriate to the panache of a guardian.

29 SEATED FEMALE FIGURE HOLDING A VESSEL

See page 16.

30 HALF-FIGURE OF A MAN ON A PRESTIGE STOOL

Mbete; southeastern Gabon or People's Republic of the Congo; late 19th–early 20th centuries
Wood, pigment, cowry shells, fiber, and metal
29 x 7½ in. (73.5 x 19 cm)

Mbete tradition housed cult relics within the image destined to guard them. Such images are thus reliquaries or reliquary figures in the strict sense. They often held the bones of notables of different clans who were members of cults concerned with hunting and other masculine activities. In this type of reliquary the torso was hollowed out from the back and covered by a hinged lid.

31 RELIQUARY SURMOUNTED
BY A POLYCHROME VERSION
OF A GUARDIAN
An undetermined people, probably
Mbamba or Ndumu; southeastern
Gabon or southwestern People's
Republic of the Congo;
20th century(?)
Wood and pigment
13¾ x 6 in. (35 x 15 cm)

The rarity of this type of reliquary
may indicate improvisation in the
absence of the metal typically used
to cover the guardian image. If so,
some irony informs the reversal: the
model with a three-dimensional head
but a two-dimensional coiffure was
doubtless a response to the technical
difficulties of laying metal over a
completely three-dimensional form.
The holes around the opening of
the body of the reliquary may have
facilitated the attachment of some
kind of lid. The sharply undercut
brow of the image occurs often in
Mbamba style. This form is made
from one piece of wood.

32 FIGURE OF A STANDING
WOMAN
An undetermined northern
Yaunde-Fang group; southwestern
Cameroun; ca. 1900(?)
Wood and pigment
27½ x 6¼ in. (70 x 16 cm)

The style and size of this statue
indicate a context different from the
melan cult of family relics. They suggest a role in the *so* initiation cycle
for young men, in which figures of
this size are either carved out of a
single log to enhance the front section of a dancing platform or carved
separately to flank the tableau as a
couple. Such statues were usually
colored with several pigments.

33 RELIQUARY GUARDIAN FIGURE

Probably a Kota-speaking people;
Upper Ogowe River region, Gabon
and People's Republic of the Congo;
possibly 19th century
Wood and metal
15¼ x 6 in. (38.5 x 15 cm)

The accession in 1884 by the Musée
d'Ethnographie du Trocadéro in Paris
of an example (attributed to the
"Ondoumbo") of this style suggests
that the tradition was established at
least by the 1870s. That example was
presumably collected in the region of
present-day Franceville. No evidence
is found for the ethnic origin of this
style or the length of its duration
into the twentieth century. Many of
the early specimens attributed to the
Ndumu ("Ondoumbo") were made in
appreciably different styles.

34 RELIQUARY GUARDIAN FIGURE

Northern Sango and possibly Tsogho
peoples; Gabon; ca. 1900(?)
Wood, pigment, and metal; eyes of
an undetermined white substance
15 x 4½ in. (38 x 11.5 cm)

Guardian figures of this sort watched
over small basketry reliquaries that
were apparently more associated
with individuals than lineages. The
reliquaries were expected to bring
good fortune to such endeavors as
travel and trade. The queuelike
coiffure reproduces a style that Du
Chaillu observed among Tsogho
women in the 1860s, noting that
when the Sango and Tsogho lived
near each other they affected the
same attire and adornment. This
form probably played an important
part in the conception of the reliquary guardians of the Kota- and
Mbete-speaking peoples.

35 STANDING FEMALE FIGURE

Probably Ewondo; southwestern
Cameroun; ca. 1900
Wood, pigment, fiber, and metal
32 x 7 in. (81.5 x 18 cm)

This tall, attenuated statue departs
markedly from the reliquary guardian
style of the Ngumba and northern
Yaunde-Fang. The treatment of
the clavicles is part of a Ngumba
tradition, while the remnants of
the Yaunde-Fang fiber bustle show
another tradition. The Ewondo,
at least, used a range of sizable
whitened statues in an initiatory
theater within the *melan* cult.

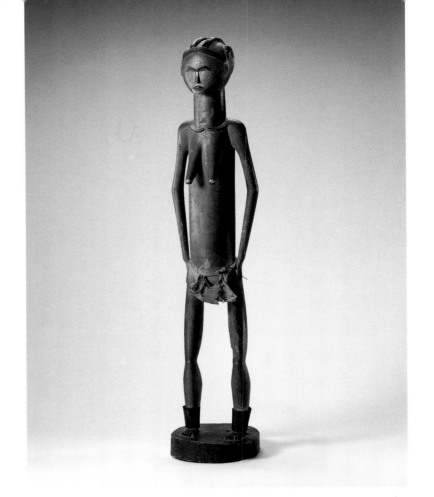

36 HALF-FIGURE OF A MAN

Tsogho; central Gabon; 20th century
Wood, pigment, and metal
9¾ x 2¾ in. (25 x 7 cm)

The Tsogho seem to have used half-
figures more than did other peoples
in the central Gabon complex. Such
images were of relatively moderate
size and were colored predominantly
red or white. Some served as reliquary guardians. Others were planted
in the floor of the temple of the main
cult where they played an important
part in dramatic nocturnal rituals.

37 FIGURE OF A WOMAN
Tsogho or Pove (Vuvi); central
Gabon; 20th century(?)
Wood, pigment, metal, and fiber
19¼ x 8½ in. (49 x 21.5 cm)

The unusual treatment of the body
and limbs of this enigmatic figure
complements the reductionist style
of the face. The striking flatness of
the body and the odd "on-point" pose
might suggest a role as a sort of mari-
onette in theatrical rites of the main
Tsogho cult.

38 STANDING FEMALE FIGURE
See page 9.

39 STANDING MAN IN STRIPED
COSTUME
An undetermined coastal people;
Gabon; possibly end of the 18th
century
Wood and pigment
17 x 6½ in. (43 x 16.5 cm)

This statue's lack of anatomical
detail might suggest that the person
represented was foreign to the
carver's society. Through the latter
part of the eighteenth century and
perhaps into the beginning of the
nineteenth century some European
sailors wore striped jerseys and
corded breeches. If this figure represents that fashion, it is likely to
have originated on the coast of
northern Gabon, where direct trading
with Europeans was intensive and
the ethnic identities of its African
participants could change considerably over a generation or two.

Men's House and Leadership Objects

40 SIDE PANELS OF AN
ALTAR FRAME
See page 14.

41 PILLAR WITH STANDING
FEMALE FIGURE
Tsogho; central Gabon; 20th century
Wood and pigment
65 x 4 in. (165 x 10 cm)

The Tsogho main cult house was
essentially a long, partly open-sided
hangarlike shelter entered through
one of the short sides. Its main
columns, those that supported the
ridgepole and the shorter ones that
bore the weight of the eaves, were
often figurated at the entrance. The
representational themes had no pre-
scribed position on the length of the
column, nor did the images express
the act of support. Styles ranged from
relative naturalism to bold conven-
tionalization. Lack of technical studies of the construction of the temple
leaves unexplained the architectonic
sense of the finial and the transverse
perforation through the bottom segment in this example.

42 PROBABLY A
COLUMN FINIAL
See page 13.

43 FIGURE OF A SEATED MAN
Yaunde-Fang group, probably Fang;
Gabon and Equatorial Guinea; ca.
1900(?)
Wood and pigment
26 x 12 in. (66 x 30.5 cm)

Figures of this kind served as bases
of the pillars that supported the roofs
of men's houses. Two or three other
examples have appeared on the market. All have been truncated at the
crown, leaving us to wonder about
the decoration of the remainder of
the pillar. Although in recognizable
Fang style, the distinctive features of
the reliquary guardian style are lack-
ing in these examples of the genre.

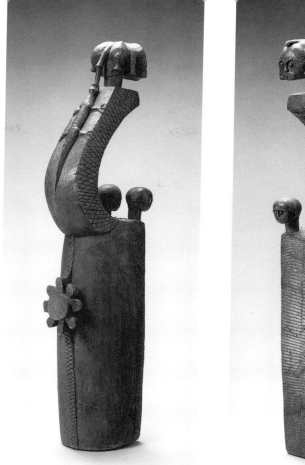

44 BOW-HARP WITH HANDLE AND RESONATOR CARVED FROM THE SAME PIECE OF WOOD

Tsogho; central Gabon; 20th century
Wood, metal, and reptile skin
29½ x 7½ in. (75 x 19 cm)

In the twentieth century the main Tsogho cult gave rise to a modern version with which it appears to have coexisted. The latter-day religion assimilated beliefs and icons from Christianity. The rosette— or sunburst—on the back of the resonator of this instrument is not a traditional motif and may indicate that the harp was made for the twentieth-century offshoot religion called Bwiti by its Western students. The integral nature of the handle and resonator is unusual. The bow, analogous to the neck of a modern European harp, is missing.

45 HEAD ON A LONG COLUMNAR NECK

Probably northern Sango; central Gabon; 20th century
Wood and pigment
10 x 4¼ in. (25.5 x 11 cm)

The length of the neck suggests its possible use as the handle of a bow-harp, the principal musical instrument of central Gabon. The ravaged neck, however, neither confirms nor denies the former existence of a pair of holes on the throat that would have served to attach the handle to the resonator. Moreover, the object seems too large for the size of bow-harp played in central Gabon.

46 Drum decorated with two masklike faces

A Shira-Punu people, probably
Lumbu; southwestern Gabon;
20th century
Wood, pigment, iron, and hide
14 x 10¼ in. (35.5 x 26 cm)

This drum falls into a short series,
apparently by one carver whose sig-
nature was a maskoid or perhaps a
rendering of a beautiful woman's face
in Shira-Punu style, reproduced two
or three times in high relief around
the upper part of a drum with slightly
concave sides. The coiffure of these
embellishments agrees with that of
masks and figures attributed to the
Lumbu. Very little is known of the
uses and contexts of Lumbu masks;
it is therefore too soon to make a
connection between this kind of
drum and the performance of a mask
similar to the faces that adorn the
drum.

47 Two-chambered bellows

Ndumu; Gabon, Franceville region;
1880s or earlier
Wood, pigment, fiber, hide, and
cowry shells
28½ x 10¾ in. (72.5 x 27.5 cm)

The Ndumu are Mbete speakers who
figured importantly in the Franceville
region's first contacts with Brazza.
They probably had a distinctive style
of metal-covered reliquary guardian,
but researchers have so far been
unable to isolate it. The Ndumu did
have a statuary style closely related
to that of the Mbete and Mbamba but
considerably more naturalistic and
gracile. This style also appeared
enhancing such utilitarian items as
these bellows. A noteworthy female
reliquary figure obtained from Brazza
and Pecile in 1889 by the Musée
d'Ethnographie du Trocadéro seems
to have been made by the same carver.

48 TOBACCO PIPE WITH
FINIAL IN THE FORM OF A
HUMAN HEAD AND NECK
An unlocalized Mbamba group;
eastcentral Gabon; 20th century
Wood and metal
20½ x 2½ in. (52 x 6.5 cm)

Some Mbamba groups carved in a
less severe, more naturalistic style,
as in the town of Otola in Okondja
District, Gabon. The continuous
(rather than cubistic) features of the
face on the finial of this pipe suggest
a relationship to the styles of this
town, which produced metal-covered
reliquary guardian figures and pairs
of charming small figures.

49 FLYWHISK WITH HANDLE
ENDING IN A BIFRONTAL
HEAD
Possibly a Kota-speaking group;
western Gabon, on and around an
island above Ndjolé, lower end of
the Middle Ogowe River; ca. 1880
Wood, pigment, and hair (buffalo tail)
13¾ (with whisk) x 2 in. (35 x 5 cm)

The Kota of the lower Middle Ogowe
River became extinct around the turn
of the century. Their name does not
necessarily relate them closely to
the larger Kota group. Around 1877
the Berlin Ethnographic Museum
acquired a flywhisk quite similar to
this one but apparently by a different
carver. The significance of these han-
dles is that they illustrate a style of
coiffure and carving that would be
ascribed to the Fang if records did
not indicate the contrary. This kind
of coiffure was widespread through
the northern Ogowe River basin from
the coast to the land of the Kwele,
at least through the latter half of
the nineteenth century.

50 SPOON WITH HANDLE IN THE FORM OF A FEMALE FIGURE

Probably northern Yaunde-Fang;
southwestern Cameroun; ca. 1900
Wood and pigment
6¼ x 2 in. (16 x 5 cm)

Elders and notables carried about
their own spoons in preparation for
communions with their peers. The
small size of these utensils reflects
an ascetic strain in Yaunde-Fang
culture. The miniaturist fretwork
characterizes northern Yaunde-Fang
decoration. The eye cavities were
intended to hold white beads.

51 SEATED MALE FIGURE WITH MISSING HANDS AND SHANKS CUT INTO PRONGS

Probably a northern Yaunde-Fang
people; northern Cameroun;
20th century
Wood, pigment, and glass
4¼ x 1 in. (11 x 2.5 cm)

The pronglike extremities seem to be
unique. Speculation includes either
damage made good in a staff-finial or
a handle of some sort, or a provision
for fixing the object upright on the
lid of a boy's training reliquary. The
large perforation across the neck
strongly suggests that originally the
figure was suspended and that the
damage and its dissimulation took
place later. No ethnographic evidence
for wearing figurines on the person
has come forth, but the possibility
is not to be dismissed.

Objects Not in Exhibition

BIFRONTAL HELMET MASK
Fang, probably a group in the Como
and Abanga River basins; westcentral
Gabon; 20th century
Wood, pigment, and fiber
14½ (mask only) x 10½ in.
(37 x 26.5 cm)

FACE MASK
Fang; Gabon, Equatorial Guinea,
southwestern Cameroun; 20th
century
Wood and pigment
16 x 9 in. (40.5 x 23 cm)

FACE MASK
Probably some Tsogho style
elements; central Gabon;
20th century
Wood, pigment, fiber, and iron
11 (mask only) x 7½ in. (28 x 19 cm)

HELMET MASK WITH
INSERTED HORNLIKE FORMS
Fang or Bulu; southcentral Cameroun
and adjacent Gabon; 20th century
Wood, pigment, fiber, and resin
25 (with horns) x 25¼ in.
(63.5 x 64 cm)

FACE MASK
Northern Sango style elements;
central Gabon; early 20th century
Wood, pigment, and fiber
13¼ x 8½ in. (33.5 x 21.5 cm)

FACE MASK
Probably Fang; Gabon or Equatorial
Guinea; 20th century
Wood and pigment
10¾ x 6 in. (27.5 x 15 cm)

MASKOID (WORN ON ARM)
Fang or Bulu; Equatorial Guinea
and adjacent parts of Gabon and
Cameroun; early 20th century
Wood
6¾ x 2¼ in. (17 x 5.5 cm)

FACE MASK
Shira-Punu; southwestern Gabon
and southwestern People's Republic
of the Congo; 20th century
Wood, pigment, and fiber
13 x 7 in. (33 x 18 cm)

SOLID HEAD WITH A
VERTICAL MEDIAN FLANGE
IN BACK
Northern Sango style elements,
possibly some Nzebi components;
central Gabon; 20th century
Wood and pigment
9 x 4¾ in. (23 x 12 cm)

FACE MASK
Nzebi; central Gabon and westcentral People's Republic of the Congo;
20th century
Wood and pigment
13¼ x 5¾ in. (33.5 x 14.5 cm)

MASK
Teke people, Tsaayi group, style of
Lékana village; central south People's
Republic of the Congo, north and
northwest of the town of Zanaga;
ca. 1960
Wood, pigment, and fiber
14¼ x 13½ in. (36 x 34 cm)

FACE MASK
Undetermined people; said to
come from Rio Muni, mainland
of Equatorial Guinea; early 20th
century(?)
Wood and pigment
13 x 10 in. (33 x 25.5 cm)

HUMAN HEAD ON
A LONG NECK
Probably Fang; Gabon, Equatorial
Guinea, southwestern Cameroun;
20th century
Wood and metal
ca. 5 x 2½ in. (12.5 x 6.5 cm)

HUMAN HEAD ON
A LONG NECK
Apparently combines northern Sango
and Nzebi style elements; central
Gabon; 20th century(?)
Wood and pigment
ca. 9¾ x 5¼ in. (29 x 13.5 cm)

FINIAL OF A STAFF
Tsogho; central Gabon; 20th century
Wood and pigment
ca. 5½ x 2½ in. (14 x 6.5 cm)

HUMAN HEAD ON HANDLE
Indeterminate style; possibly central
Gabon; probably 20th century
Wood, pigment, and fiber
5½ (head only) x 2½ in. (14 x 6.5 cm)

HALF-FIGURE OF A
MAN ON A PEDESTAL
Fang; probably a group in eastern
Equatorial Guinea; 20th century(?)
Wood and pigment
13 x 4½ in. (33 x 11.5 cm)

FIGURE OF A STANDING
WOMAN
An undetermined people, conceivably Fang; Equatorial Guinea(?);
20th century
Wood and pigment
17¼ x 5 in. (44 x 12.5 cm)

MINIATURE FORK AND
SPOON WITH HUMAN
FIGURES AS FINIALS
Tsogho; central Gabon; 20th century
Wood and pigment
Spoon 5½ x 1 in. (14 x 2.5 cm),
Fork 4¾ x¾ in. (12 x 2 cm)

RELIQUARY GUARDIAN
FIGURE
Hongwe, Shamaye, and probably
other Kota-speaking peoples; Gabon;
Ivindo River basin, People's Republic
of the Congo; probably 20th century
Wood and metal
ca. 12¾ x 5 in. (32.5 x 12.5 cm)

METAL COLLARS
Fang, Kwele, and other peoples;
Gabon, Equatorial Guinea, and
Cameroun; late 19th and early
20th century
Metal
A 5¾ in. (14.5 cm) diam., B 5¾ in.
(14.5 cm) diam., C 4¾ in. (12 cm)
diam., D 6½ in. (16.5 cm) diam.

BRIDEWEALTH MONEY
IN THE FORM OF AN
EXAGGERATED AXE BLADE
Kwele, eastern group; People's
Republic of the Congo; late
19th–early 20th century
Metal
20¼ x 15¼ in. (51.5 x 38.5 cm)

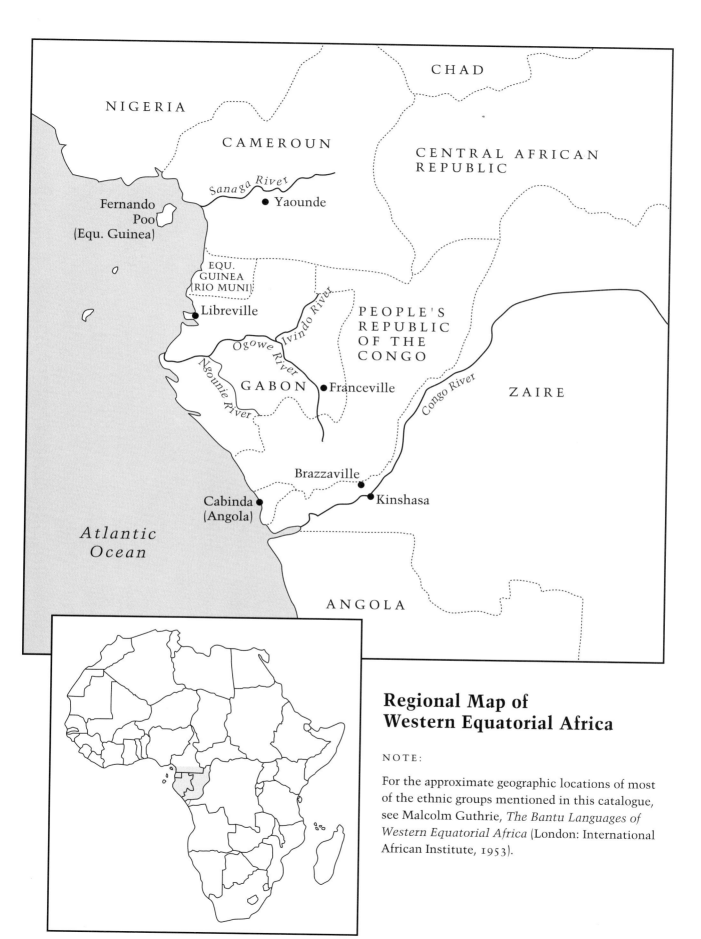

CHAD

NIGERIA

CAMEROUN

CENTRAL AFRICAN
REPUBLIC

Sanaga River

● Yaounde

Fernando
Poo
(Equ. Guinea)

EQU.
GUINEA
(RIO MUNI)

● Libreville

Ogowe River

Ivindo River

PEOPLE'S
REPUBLIC
OF THE
CONGO

Ngounie River

GABON

● Franceville

Congo River

ZAIRE

Brazzaville
●

*Atlantic
Ocean*

Cabinda
(Angola) ●

● Kinshasa

ANGOLA

Regional Map of
Western Equatorial Africa

NOTE:

For the approximate geographic locations of most
of the ethnic groups mentioned in this catalogue,
see Malcolm Guthrie, *The Bantu Languages of
Western Equatorial Africa* (London: International
African Institute, 1953).

NEW DIRECTIONS FOR THE ARTS OF EQUATORIAL AFRICA

Alisa LaGamma

In presenting new approaches that may advance the appreciation of Equatorial Africa's artistic heritage, it is necessary to consider the intellectual frameworks used to examine it in the past. To date, emphasis has primarily been placed on the study of formal qualities and the establishment of stylistic attributions. The consequence of prevailing attitudes has been the casting of objects in molds that suggest static identities. A forest of theoretical concerns has grown up around them, however. In light of the fluid nature of regional cultural interaction and exchange systems, such categorization appears especially contrived. As the field of African art history develops, it becomes evident that beyond the formal appeal of these arts lie equally exciting systems of belief and ideological content.

On a practical level, one of the major obstacles to research in this region is the impenetrability of its terrain. The landscape of open plains engulfed by dense rain forest is also permeated by thousands of waterways, ranging from streams and rivulets to rivers, almost all of which are unnavigable. To a certain extent this geographic fragmentation has contributed to the Western perception that the region is characterized by a multiplicity of small and disconnected cultural entities. Consequently, emphasis has been placed on determining provenance of objects as if they were shaped entirely by site-specific conventions. Now that several generations of scholars have pursued findings based on extended field research in adjacent ethnic areas, we are engaged in reexamining the interpretative approaches taken in the past as well as broadening the parameters of our concerns.

Among the avenues that would further the understanding of a history of Equatorial African art history are the exploration of thematic issues that cross ethnic boundaries, continued pursuit of contemporary field studies that document newly developing contexts for artistic expression, reexamination of previously recognized traditions whose significance has been overlooked, and efforts to understand local criteria for appreciating art forms and their roles within local systems of power.

Rather than focus upon determining stylistic differences and constructing formal boundaries, I would propose that we consider the shared ideas that have been translated into artistically distinctive forms. For example, both the highly abstract and rectilinear Mbete or Mbamba mask (cat. no. 18) and the comparatively naturalistically modeled Shira-Punu mask (cat. no. 25) may be performed in similar contexts, such as an event that celebrates the birth of twins. The practice of dancing on stilts that is characteristic of the interior Punu today is also documented as being performed on the coast at Port-Gentil in the 1830s.

The coherence of a conceptual system that draws together what have come to be classified as many disparate ethnic traditions is also apparent in a broadly based language of color. Within it, a vocabulary of red, white, and black is applied to the surface of masks and architectural sculpture, as well as the bodies of initiates into various healing societies. In her study *Red-White-Black as a Mode of Thought,* Anita Jacobson-Widding considers color as a key to an entire system of symbolic representation produced by cultures of Equatorial Africa. Accordingly, these colors correspond to basic principles of cosmic and social order and can be read both as single signs and as elements in relationship to other symbols.[1]

The historian Jan Vansina has noted that in the nineteenth century two-thirds of Equatorial Africa was organized into trading networks that would effectively exploit interior resources for exchange at the coast.[2] Within these networks art objects found their way into the hands of European traders. A clearer picture of precolonial and colonial commercial interactions would contribute to understanding the manner in which artistic forms have been appropriated and transformed. This phenomenon has been documented to a certain extent in the case of a regional religious movement known as Bwiti.

Bwiti, as a Fang synchretic religion that fuses elements of Christianity with precolonial African beliefs, has been the focus of a great deal of scholarly attention. Although a dominant force in contemporary Fang culture, according to oral traditions it originated in a remote area of southcentral Gabon among the Tsogho. As the influence of Bwiti continues to grow and expand throughout contemporary Gabon, regional studies by a range of scholars, including Fernandez, Gollnhofer, and Swiderski, contribute to the understanding of an ongoing tradition of sculptural forms produced for ritual contexts.[3] Other more transitory religious movements have similarly been responsible for the patronage of certain art forms. Often the focus of these ephemeral regional associations is described as a power that is embodied in a concrete sacred object.

Contemporary fieldwork offers opportunities to discern the development of new contexts for artistic patronage. A comparative perspective that takes into account the legacy of sculptural traditions also allows appreciation of how their identities may become reconfigured. In my own research in Gabon and the People's Republic of the Congo on the Punu masquerade tradition, *mukudj,* I found that masks in a style collected in the West for over a century continue to be performed publicly for celebratory occasions. Before national independence in 1960, mask performances were incorporated within events choreographed by colonial administrators. More recently they have come to be featured at modern political rallies.[4]

Not only do Punu masks continue to be actively performed, they have been adapted locally to decorative ends as well. In a manner suggestive of European colonial practices of display, they are prominently placed over doorways and on the sitting room walls of modern Punu homes. This practice in turn affects the formal character of objects produced for such uses. They may, for example, be smaller in scale than those designed to be worn by a dancer. Paintings similarly reflecting local systems of belief, by contemporary regional artists, are also being displayed in homes.

Although past studies have addressed the idea of the active agency of sculptures in dynamic performance, this role has generally been overshadowed by formal concerns. The shiny, reflective, oiled surfaces characteristic of Fang sculptures admired for their visual effect are discussed by James Fernandez in terms of the association of ritual and sculpture (cat. no. 29, p. 16). He points out that processes performed upon initiates' bodies were replicated upon the surface of sculpture of the *byéri* cult of ancestors.[5] Because of their identification as reliquaries, however, these objects became associated with immobility. Fernandez notes that, according to the early ethnographer Günter Tessmann, sculptures were manipulated in performance by initiates concealed behind a raffia barrier. What he describes as a puppet show of sorts was presented before the entire community with figures that "danced and frolicked" to the accompaniment of drums and xylophones.

Fernandez's examination of *byéri* sculptures highlights the differences in criteria used to evaluate them by the Fang and Western collectors. Whereas the focus of interest in the West emphasized figural sculpture, in Fang culture such figures apparently served as mere accessories or complements to a reliquary container whose contents embodied cult mysteries. Due to the manner in which such objects were collected as independent entities, a range of misperceptions regarding their identity have reigned. According to Fernandez, "the ancestor figure was only their simulacrum." Consequently, the cultural legacy that Western scholars now attempt to reconstruct is often derived from locally discarded fragments and extant examples reflecting collectors' preferences. Such limitations imposed by collecting practices are of course not unique to Equatorial Africa. Throughout the continent, Western collecting has focused upon figural sculpture in durable materials such as wood, ivory, and metal. For example, often when masks were collected, the invariably extensive complementary costumes were not acquired.

Another common misinterpretation has been that the focus of *byéri* addressed a generalized category of ancestors at large. According to Fernandez, "the Fang did not negotiate with all the ancestors on a corporate basis but as far as possible with particular ones about whom something was known." When the memory of an ancestor incorporated within the reliquary faded, he was replaced with someone more recent and therefore more receptive. Thus, counter to Western assumptions about the qualities of timelessness and abstraction of these sculptural traditions, the Fang have always placed a premium upon their efficacy as individualized agents of change. (This also became apparent in my research on *mukudj* masks, which are conceived of as portraits that capture an individual's features in exacting detail.)

Whereas the role of Fang figural sculpture was considered to be part of the context of their religious practices—Fernandez's primary concern—one of the lacunae in African art history is the complete absence of any studies on Fang masquerade traditions. These masks, collected contemporaneously with figural sculpture, are also well known formally because of their appeal to modernists. Due to the haphazard, idiosyncratic manner of studying regional artistic traditions, only passing mention of these masks appears in an ethnographic study by Jacques Binet. During a year of field research in a related region I saw evidence that they continue to be performed in contemporary Gabon.

Leon Siroto's study of Bakwele masking practices provides a significant departure within African art history. Although the art of masquerade performance in Africa had been discussed as a means whereby the empowered reinforce their influence in society, Siroto sees it as "an implement to attain, rather than maintain, leadership."[6] It is described as a strategy for acquiring material wealth and prestige within an intensely competitive environment.

My own research on the Punu further expands the notion that regional artistic traditions are integrally tied to local discourse on the nature of power. In the case of Punu *mukudj* performance, the dancer of the mask has engaged in negotiations with a formidable force that enables him to accrue necessary mystical powers that are translated into extraordinary physical movements. The price of a dancer's excellence and ambition, however, seems to manifest in symptoms of sickness afflicting members of the community.[7] Such transactions whereby individuals derive formidable power through sorcery are often considered analogous to processes whereby wealth is accumulated through trade. Although colonial trade networks are no longer extant, the status accorded masquerade performers remains intact.

In her consideration of the contemporary arts in Africa, Susan Vogel appeals for an expansion of the scope of our vision to embrace a dynamic present. In doing so, Vogel develops categories of contemporaneous art forms that reflect different kinds of patronage. She provides a provocative case for the consideration of new strains of creative efforts by juxtaposing categories of "new functional art," "urban art," and "international art" with that of "extinct art."[8]

According to Vogel's system, objects of the type presented in the Strong Collection—referred to as "traditional art of the past"—would fall into the "extinct art" grouping. While Vogel recognizes that these artistic traditions have undeniable significance for contemporary creativity in Africa on many levels, ranging from local to ethnic to national, and although she acknowledges that these arts continue to be produced, she nonetheless relegates them to a realm of obsolescence because they were conceived in a precolonial era. This attempt at categorization, however, like those that emphasize stylistic formalism, fails to capture and reflect the continued immediacy with which these art forms still respond to contemporary realities while thoughtfully drawing upon their own art history.

NOTES

1. Anita Jacobson-Widding, *Red-White-Black as a Mode of Thought* (Stockholm: Acta Universitatis Upsaliensis, 1979).

2. Jan Vansina, *Paths in the Rainforests* (Madison: University of Wisconsin Press, 1990).

3. James W. Fernandez, *Bwiti: An Ethnography of the Religious Imagination in Africa* (Princeton: Princeton University Press, 1982); Otto Gollnhofer and Roger Sillans, "Symbolisme et prophylaxie chez les Mitsogho," *Anthropos* 73 (1978): 449–460; Otto Gollnhofer and Roger Sillans, "Phénoménologie de la possession chez les Mitsogho," *Psychopathologie africaine* 10, no. 2 (1974): 187–209; Otto Gollnhofer and Roger Sillans, "Recherche sur le mysticisme des Mitsogho," in *Réincarnation et vie mystique en Afrique noire* (Paris: Strasbourg Colloquium, 1965), 143–173; Stanislaw Swiderski, "Le Bwiti, société d'initiation chez les Apindji au Gabon," *Anthropos* 60 (1965): 541–576.

4. Alisa LaGamma, "The Punu *Mukudj* Masquerade: The Dance of a Living Memory" (Ph.D. diss., Columbia University, n.d.).

5. Fernandez, *Bwiti.* Fernandez uses the spelling *"bieri."*

6. Leon Siroto, *Masks and Social Organization among the BaKwele People of Western Equatorial Africa* (Ann Arbor, Mich.: University Microfilms, 1970), 1.

7. Alisa LaGamma, "Unimaginable Sacrifices: The Allure of *Muyama*" (paper presented at the annual meeting of the African Studies Association, Toronto, 1994).

8. Susan Vogel, *Africa Explores: Twentieth Century African Art,* exh. cat. (New York: The Center for African Art, 1991).

SELECTED BIBLIOGRAPHY

Alisa LaGamma

Colonial Sources:

Brazza, Pierre Savorgnan de. "Voyages dans l'ouest Africain." *Le Tour du monde* 44 (1877): 289–336; 45 (1888): 1–25.

Du Chaillu, Paul B. *A Journey to Ashango-land and Further Penetration into Equatorial Africa.* New York: Harper, 1874.

———. *Explorations and Adventures in Equatorial Africa.* New York: Harper, 1861.

———. *My Apindji Kingdom.* New York: Harper, 1871.

———. *The Country of the Dwarfs.* New York: Harper, 1872.

Kingsley, Mary. *Travels in West Africa: Congo Français, Corisco, and Cameroons.* New York: Macmillan, 1897.

Nassau, Robert Hamill. *My Ogowe: Being a Narrative of Daily Incidents during Sixteen Years in Equatorial West Africa.* New York: Neale, 1914.

Tessmann, Günter. "Verlauf und Ergebnisse der Lübecker Pangwe Expedition." *Globus* 97, no. 1 (1910): 1–10; no. 2 (1910): 25–29.

———. *Die Pangwe: Völkerkundliche Monographie eines westafrikanischen Negerstammes.* 2 vols. Berlin: Ernst Wasmuth, 1913.

Trilles, H. "Proverbes, légendes, et contes fang." *Bulletin de la société neufchatelloise de géographie* 16 (1905): 49–295.

———. *Totemisme chez le Fang.* Münster, W. Ger.: Bibliothèque-Anthropos, 1912.

———. *Les pygmées de la forêt équatoriale.* Paris: Bloud, 1932.

Art and Stylistic Studies:

Chaffin, Alain. "Art kota." *Arts d'Afrique noire* 5 (1973): 12–43.

———. "Complément d'information sur `L'art kota.'" *Arts d'Afrique noire* 33 (1980): 42–43.

Chaffin, Alain, and Françoise Chaffin. *L'art kota.* Meudon: Chaffin, 1979.

Fourquet, André. "Chefs-d'oeuvre de l'Afrique: Les masques pounou." *L'Oeil, revue d'art mensuelle* 321 (1982): 52–57.

Goldwater, Robert. *The Great Bieri.* New York: The Museum of Primitive Art, 1962.

Lehuard, Raoul. "Arts Bakongo: Les centres de style." *Arts d'Afrique noire,* supp. 55 (1989), 2 vols.

McKesson, John. "Réflexions sur la sculpture des reliquaires fang." *Arts d'Afrique noire* 62 (1987): 2–21.

Perrois, Louis. "Aspects de la sculpture traditionnelle du Gabon." *Anthropos* 63/64, no. 5 (1968–69): 869–888.

———. Gabon: *Culture et techniques.* Libreville, Gabon: ORSTOM, 1969.

———. "L'art kota-mahongwe: Les figures funéraires du bassin de l'Ivindo (Gabon-Congo)." *Arts d'Afrique noire* 20 (1976): 15–37.

———. *Problèmes d'analyse de la sculpture traditionnelle.* Paris: ORSTOM, 1977.

———. *Arts du Gabon.* Arnouville: Arts d'Afrique noire, 1979.

———. *The Art of Equatorial Guinea: The Fang.* New York: Rizzoli, 1990.

Siroto, Leon. "Notes on the Bakota, Pangwe, and Balumbo Sculpture of the Gabon and the Middle Congo." In *Masterpieces of African Art.* New York: Brooklyn Museum, 1955.

———. "The Face of the Bwiti." *African Arts/Arts d'Afrique* 1, no. 3 (1968): 22–27.

Siroto, Leon, and Irwin Child. "Bakwele and American Esthetic Evaluations Compared." *Ethnology* 18 (1965): 349–360.

Art History/Anthropology:

Andersson, Efraim. *Contribution à l'ethnographie des Kuta.* 3 vols. Uppsala, Swed.: Almqvist & Wiksell, 1953–91.

Binet, Jacques. *Sociétés de danse chez les Fang du Gabon.* Paris: ORSTOM, 1972.

Chauvet, Stephen. "L'art funéraire au Gabon." *Bulletin des Soeurs de Notre Dame de l'Immaculée Conception/Soeurs Bleues de Castres* 8 (January 1933): 6–11.

Cinnamon, John. "The Long March of the Fang." Ph.D. diss., Yale University, n.d.

Collomb, Gerard. "Métallurgie du cuivre et circulation des biens dans le Gabon précoloniale." *Objets et mondes* 18, 1/2 (1978): 59–68.

Dupré, Marie-Claude. "Art et histoire chez les Teke tsaayi du Congo." *Antologia di belle arti* 5, no. 17/18 (1981): 105–128.

———. "Masques de danse ou cartes géopolitiques: L'invention de Kidumu chez les Teke tsayi au XIXe siècle (République populaire du Congo)." *Cahiers de Sciences humaines* 26, no. 3 (1990): 447–471.

———. "Colours in Kidumu Masks of the Teke Tsaayi." In *Body and Space: Symbolic Models of Unity and Division in African Cosmology and Experience,* ed. Anita Jacobson-Widding. Stockholm: Uppsala Studies in Cultural Anthropology, 1991.

Fernandez, James W. "Principles of Opposition and Vitality in Fang Aesthetics." *The Journal of Aesthetics and Art Criticism* 25 (1966): 53–64.

———. "The Affirmation of Things Past: Alar Ayong and Bwiti as Movements of Protest in Central and Northern Gabon." In *Protest and Power in Black Africa,* ed. R. Rotberg and A. Mazrui, 339–366. New York: Oxford University Press, 1970.

———. "Fang Representations under Acculturation." In *Africa and the Intellectual Responses to European Culture,* ed. Philip Curtin, 3–48. Madison: University of Wisconsin Press, 1972.

———. "The Exposition and Imposition of Order: Artistic Expression in Fang Culture." In *The Traditional Artist in African Societies*, ed. W. L. d'Azevedo, 194–220. Bloomington: Indiana University Press, 1973.

———. *Bwiti: An Ethnography of the Religious Imagination in Africa*. Princeton: Princeton University Press, 1982.

Fernandez, James W., and Renate Fernandez, "Fang Reliquary Art: Its Quantities and Qualities." *Cahiers d'études africaines* 15, no. 4 (1975): 723–746.

Gollnhofer, Otto, Pierre Sallée, and Roger Sillans. *Art et artisanat tsogho*. Paris: ORSTOM, 1975.

Gollnhofer, Otto, and Roger Sillans. "Phénomènologie de la possession chez les Mitsogho (Gabon): Rites et techniques." *Anthropos* 74, no. 5/6 (1979): 737–752.

———. "Essai d'approche du concept et du mécanisme des objets-médiateurs chez les Mitsogho (Gabon)." In *Ethnologiques: Hommages à Marcel Griaule*, ed. Solange de Ganay, 157–165. Paris: Hermann, 1987.

LaGamma, Alisa. "Unimaginable Sacrifices: The Allure of *Muyama*." Paper presented at the annual meeting of the African Studies Association, Toronto, 1994.

———. "The Punu *Mukudj* Masquerade: The Dance of a Living Memory." Ph.D. diss., Columbia University, n.d.

Millot, Jacques. "De Pointe-Noire au pays Tsogo." *Objets et mondes* 1, no. 3/4 (1961): 65–80.

Raponda-Walker, André, and Roger Sillans. *Rites et croyances des peuples du Gabon*. Paris: Présence Africaine, 1962.

Siroto, Leon. *Masks and Social Organization among the BaKwele People of Western Equatorial Africa*. Ann Arbor, Mich.: University Microfilms, 1970.

———. "Gon: A Mask Used in Competition for Leadership among the BaKwele." In *African Art and Leadership*, ed. Douglas Fraser and Herbert M. Cole. Madison: University of Wisconsin Press, 1972.

———. "Njom: The Magical Bridge of the Beti and Buli of Southern Cameroon." *African Arts* 10, no. 2 (1977): 38–51; 90–91.

———. "Das westliche Aequatorial-Afrika." In *Kunst der Naturvölker*, ed. Elsy Leuzinger. Berlin: Propylaen Verlag, 1978.

———. "Postscript on Njom." *African Arts* 11, no. 3 (1978): 86–87.

———. "Witchcraft Belief in the Explanation of Traditional African Iconography." In *The Visual Arts: Plastic and Graphic*, ed. Justine M. Cordwell. The Hague: Mouton, 1979.

———. "Western Equatorial Africa." In *Spoons in African Art: Cooking, Serving, Eating, Emblems of Abundance*, ed. Lorenz Homburger. Zurich: Museum Rietberg, 1991.

Swiderski, Stanislaw. "La harpe sacrée dans les cultes syncrétiques au Gabon." *Anthropos* 65 (1970): 831–857.

———. "Le symbolisme du poteau central Gabon." *Mitteilungen der Anthropologischen Gesellschaft*, Band C (1970): 299–315.

———. "L'Ombwiri: Société d'initiation et de guérison au Gabon." *Religione e Civiltá*. Vol. 1. Rome: Dedalo Libri, 1974.

———. "Le rite de la renaissance spirituelle dans la religion Bouiti (Gabon)." *Anthropos* 73, no. 5/6 (1978): 845–886.

———. "Tradition et nouveauté des concepts religieux dans l'art sacré contemporain au Gabon." *Anthropos* 74, no. 5/6 (1979): 803–816.

History:

Ambouroue-Avaro, Joseph. *Un peuple gabonais à l'aube de la colonisation: le Bas-Ogowe au XIXe siècle.* Paris: Centre de Recherches africaines, 1981.

Birmingham, David, and Phyllis M. Martin, eds. *History of Central Africa.* 2 vols. London: Longham, 1983.

Deschamps, Hubert Jules. *Traditions orales et archives au Gabon: Contribution à l'ethno-histoire.* Paris: Berger-Levrault, 1962.

Gray, Christopher. "The Disappearing District: The Decline of Precolonial Space in Southern Gabon, 1850–1940." Paper presented at the annual meeting of the African Studies Association, Toronto, 1994.

———. "Who Does Historical Research in Gabon? Obstacles to the Development of a Scholarly Tradition." *History in Africa* 21 (1994): 413–433.

———. "Territoriality, Ethnicity, and Colonial Rule in Southern Gabon, 1850–1960." Ph.D. diss., Indiana University, n.d.

Martin, Phyllis M. *The External Trade of the Loango Coast.* Oxford: Oxford University Press, 1972.

Vansina, Jan. *Paths in the Rainforests.* Madison: University of Wisconsin Press, 1990.

Exhibition Catalogues:

Perrois, Louis. *Les côtes d'Afrique équatoriale il y a 100 ans,* exh. cat. Caen: Musée des Beaux-Arts, 1983.

———. *Ancestral Art of Gabon from the Collections of the Barbier-Mueller Museum,* exh. cat. Geneva: Musée Barbier-Mueller, 1985.

———. *Byéri Fang: Sculptures d'ancêtres en Afrique,* exh. cat. Marseille: Musée de Marseille, 1992.